EVERYDAY
PRAYERS
— FOR —
PEACE

A 30-Day Devotional & Reflective Journal for Women

WHITAKER
HOUSE

Everyday Prayers for Peace
A 30-Day Devotional & Reflective Journal for Women

www.millionprayingmoms.com
brookemcglothlin.net

ISBN: 978-1-64123-890-8
eBook ISBN: 978-1-64123-891-5
Printed in the United States of America
© 2022 by Brooke McGlothlin

Whitaker House
1030 Hunt Valley Circle
New Kensington, PA 15068
www.whitakerhouse.com

Library of Congress Control Number: 2022945855

1 2 3 4 5 6 7 8 9 10 11 ᴜᴜ 29 28 27 26 25 24 23 22

CONTENTS

FOREWORD

Peace in the Bible is not merely the absence of war, but the presence of wholeness. When we see the word *shalom*, it connotes a robust, wholehearted fullness of body, mind, and spirit. It's what God provides for a mother in the trenches, whether she's an exasperated chef to many, an exhausted caregiver, or up to her ears in dirty laundry. God is the source of this *shalom*, and He readily grants it to those in need.

To ask for peace like that is to pray. I can think of no other person to best pen a book about prayer and peace and parenthood than Brooke McGlothlin. She has walked the journey from joy to heartache back to fullness again. She's a companion alongside the roadway of motherhood, encouraging from a position of empathy.

I have not always parented with peace. Having grown up in a home I didn't want to duplicate, I feared I would not do parenting right because I had so little to draw from. My motherhood sprang from desperation and a longing to love my kids well despite my inadequacies. So often, in the midst of the chaos of a home full of children, I would give in to exasperation.

In the evening, I would recount all my parental failures, berating myself for not measuring up to an artificial standard I had created. This, my friend, was not peace.

The one thing I did do well, though, was cry. And often those tears were directed heavenward in a sort of desperate prayer for help. I knew my lack. I knew my insecurities. I knew my inabilities. This knowledge became a gift for me.

Why? Because my lack propelled me into the arms of Jesus, who was utterly capable of helping me thrive as a mom. Eventually, I realized that He wasn't tasking me with the impossible (creating peace in our home), but He was equipping me to be a person of peace in the midst of the mess. In short, He steadied me. He gave me hope. Through the Holy Spirit within, He granted me long-suffering patience and a quieter voice. He helped me see my children as fellow strugglers along the pathway of life, giving me empathy for them.

If I could summarize my favorite parenting verse, it would be an odd one:

> *So now I am glad to boast about my weaknesses, so that the power of Christ can work through me. That's why I take pleasure in my weaknesses, and in the insults, hardships, persecutions, and troubles that I suffer for Christ. For when I am weak, then I am strong.* —2 Corinthians 12:9–10 NLT

I learned peace didn't emanate from me in my own strength; it was created on the stage of my weakness and insecurity. True *shalom* in my home came when I understood my deep need for Jesus, and I asked Him to help me love my children.

There is joy in knowing we don't have to manufacture the very peace Jesus wants to give us when we cry out from our knees in weakness.

—*Mary E. Demuth*
Author, *The Beautiful Word for Christmas*
Podcaster, *Pray Every Day*

INTRODUCTION

ON PEACE

One of the hardest parts of parenting in an all-boy home, at least for me, is the noise. I'm an introvert mom to a mix of personalities (introvert and extrovert boys), and wife to a husband who is probably best described as living somewhere in between. What this means, in a very real way for me, is that home can be *hard*. The noise simply never stops…unless they're asleep. It's been this way for years. My sons are now teenagers, so I have to assume this might not be something that goes away. Sometimes, when I hear my youngest beatboxing absent-mindedly while walking through the house, I think I'll miss it one day, but the truth is that one of the things I value most in life is simple peace and quiet. I just don't get enough of it.

It took me years to realize that introverts aren't being selfish when they say they need time alone, time to just be quiet. Our personalities demand it. Actually, I think it's safe to say our bodies themselves demand it. If I go too long in "on" mode, I'll start to develop a headache. It's like my body—my very physical, biological, and spiritual makeup—starts to shut down and force me to get away.

Moms of girls, I know your homes can be just as loud as the boy homes are—the noises are just different, right? Even empty nesters and those without children can struggle with feeling overwhelmed by the noises of their lives. I can't tell you how many times I've pleaded with my family over the years to just give me a few minutes of peace. But I've come to realize that my peace doesn't have to depend on what's happening around me. Peace is not just quiet, although it can be that. Peace is an internal state that belongs to me as a child of God—a Jesus follower—that was sealed and called indestructible the day I gave my life to Christ. Literally nothing can take it away!

Why? Because the Scriptures say Jesus Himself *is* our peace.

Ephesians 2:14 (NLT) says, *"For Christ himself has brought peace to us. He united Jews and Gentiles into one people when, in his own body on the cross, he broke down the wall of hostility that separated us."* This verse is part of a passage where Paul is helping the church at Ephesus understand that they are no longer divided into camps. Jesus, by the shedding of His blood, literally made them *"into one people."* This is important to us because most people reading this right now, myself included, fall into the gentile camp. We were not God's original chosen people—the Jews were—but because of Jesus, we who *"were far away from God* [not the chosen race]...*have been brought near to him through the blood of Christ"* (verse 13 NLT).

We now have access to the blessings of being God's children just like the Jewish people did in the Old Testament. Once we didn't. Now we do. Praise God!

But there's more! Jesus's death on the cross didn't only serve to bring peace between Jews and gentiles. Jesus Himself is the reason *anyone* can have peace with God.

There was a time when the blessing of salvation wasn't mine. During that time, I lived at odds with God. Actually, Scripture says I lived in direct opposition to Him and deserved eternal punishment for it. But all that changed when I was about nine years old. One evening, at our church's revival service, I gave my life to Jesus and asked Him to save me from my sins. Now, because of what Jesus did for me, I have peace with God. The wrath of God in response to my sin no longer lies on my own head. Jesus took it for me. When I placed my faith in what Jesus did on the cross to pay the punishment for my sin, I gained forgiveness, an eternal home in heaven, and peace with God.

In a very real sense, we experience both momentary peace and eternal peace throughout our lives. Of course, the feelings of peace we experience in those moments when everything is going our way really are fleeting, dependent on circumstances. But eternal peace? This is the thing God seals in our heart when we come to know His Son. If we know Him, we have peace not even the worst of circumstances (or the loudest of families) can take away.

And perhaps one of the most important things about this eternal peace we have because of salvation is that it leads to mastery over the lack of momentary peace. When we see the true value of peace with God, it overshadows every other kind of noise the world might throw our way. When we recognize that our greatest need is *peace with God through the forgiveness of our sins* and know in our hearts that no circumstance, good or bad, can take that peace away, every other noise that would try to steal it fades. We can then live in the calm assurance that if our greatest need has already been met through Jesus, every other need will be met according to the riches of God at the right time.

I've chosen the verses in this prayer journal in hopes that they will help you put into practice the art of allowing your eternal peace to trump momentary attacks against it. All it takes is some effort to replace negative thoughts and emotions with trust, ask the right questions, and keep the value of your salvation the lens through which you see everything else.

To *your* peace,
Brooke McGlothlin

THE THINK, PRAY, PRAISE METHOD OF DAILY PRAYER

When I first started praying for my own children, I was inspired by two important truths about God's Word:

1. *The word of God is living and active, sharper than any two-edged sword, piercing to the division of soul and of spirit, of joints and of marrow, and discerning the thoughts and intentions of the heart.* (Hebrews 4:12)

2. God declares, *"My word that goes out from my mouth...shall not return to me empty, but it shall accomplish that which I purpose, and shall succeed in the thing for which I sent it"* (Isaiah 55:11).

If those two verses were true—and I believed they were—then it seemed to me that there could be no better thing to pray than God's Word itself! Because this experience was so deeply profound for me, it's the same one I've used to teach other women to pray. I call it my "Think, Pray, Praise" method. It isn't really rocket science, just a practical, biblical way to pray the Word of God over yourself or the people you love. It's also the method we use in Million Praying Moms' Everyday Prayers journal library. Let me walk you through it step by step.

THINK

On each daily page, we give you a verse to pray to make it easy for you to follow this prayer method. However, you can always search the Scriptures for yourself to find a verse you'd like to pray instead. After you've chosen it, reflect on, process, and meditate over your verse. If you have time, read a few verses that come before and after your verse, or even the entire chapter of the Bible so you can have the proper context from which to understand it. Consider what God is speaking to your heart through His Word and through this verse. Dream about the future and what it might look like to see the message of this verse come to fruition in your life, or in your children's lives. In a small way, analyze the verse and figure out what you're inspired to pray.

PRAY

For almost ten years, my desire has been to allow my prayers to be inspired by God's Word. I try very hard not to take verses out of context, or use them for a purpose or meaning other than that which God intended for them. Reading the verse in context, as I just suggested, really helps with this. Once I've selected a verse, I craft it into a prayer. I usually stay as word-for-word as I can and then pray that verse back to God. You can see an example of a "Verse of the Day" and the prayer we craft from it for you on the daily pages of this journal.

Once you have your verse and prayer, use your thoughts about them as a jumping-off point to allow God's Word to move you and shape your prayers.

PRAISE

Praise is my favorite part of this method of prayer! Praising God is like putting on a pair of rose-colored glasses; it literally changes the way you see the world around you.

New York Times bestselling author Ann Voskamp writes:

The brave who focus on all things good and all things beautiful and all things true, even in the small, who give thanks for it and discover joy even in the here and now, they are the change agents who bring the fullest light to all the world. Being joyful isn't what makes you grateful. Being grateful is what makes you joyful.[1]

When we pause to deliberately reflect on the good things God is doing in our lives right now, it changes everything. (This can be even the tiniest of things we have to look hard to see, like having to clean for a Bible study group in your home. You might not want to clean, but at least you have people coming over to discuss the Word of God with you!) Instead of focusing on all we don't have or don't like (such as cleaning), gratitude for what we do have (being with brothers and sisters in Christ) blossoms in our hearts, truly making us joyful. Each day, I try to write down just a few things I'm grateful for, praising God for His continuous work of grace in my life.

BONUS

You might notice the lines for a to-do list on the daily pages. I love that little block because I find that when I sit down to pray, my mind gets flooded by all the things I need to do that day. Every. Single. Time. I feel the urgency of my schedule begin to take over, distracting me from the time I so desperately need in God's Word and prayer. Taking a minute to jot down my to-do list before I get started is kind of like doing a brain dump each day. If my list is written down, I won't forget what I have to do that day. This frees me up to spend the time I've allocated in prayer without worry stealing it from me.

PRAYER REQUESTS

Part of being a woman of prayer is interceding on behalf of others. My life literally changed the day a good friend held my hands in hers and said, "Let's pray about this now," instead of telling me, "I'll pray for you." You won't always be able to pray for others in person, but

---

1. Ann Voskamp, *One Thousand Gifts: A Dare to Live Fully Right Where You Are* (Nashville, TN: W Publishing Group, 2010).

keeping track of their needs on a prayer list like the one at the bottom left of the daily pages is a great way to make sure you're being faithful to cover them in prayer.

GO!

I am so excited about the journey of prayer you hold in your hands. Each day begins with a devotion written specifically for you, and concludes with extra verses and questions for reflection that are a perfect way to take your study of joy to the next level or use with a group. We now consider you part of our Million Praying Moms family!

Connect with us at www.millionprayingmoms.com and keep us posted about the things God is doing in your life as you pray.

Day 1

WHERE DO WE REALLY GET PEACE?

READ JOHN 16

I have said these things to you, that in me you may have peace.
In the world you will have tribulation.
But take heart; I have overcome the world.
—John 16:33

I have a friend who doesn't speak plainly. He talks fast, laughs while he talks, and to top it off, he whispers. Several years ago, I had an ear issue that left me with some hearing loss, so you can imagine how hard it is for me when I'm talking to this friend. Many times, I have wanted to put my hand up and say, "Could you please just speak plainly?" It's not like he's speaking in riddles, although his sense of humor is sometimes lost on me. He's just hard for me to understand, especially in a crowd. I would never hurt his feelings by bringing it up. Instead, when we're together, I just lean in, watch his lips closely, and, sometimes, discreetly cup my ear so I can hear him better.

The Gospels paint a picture in which the twelve apostles were constantly leaning in, watching Jesus closely, and trying to hear Him better so they could understand. I imagine them sitting as close as possible, hands cupped to their ears, minds trying to absorb the true meaning of His words, which, to be honest, were a little difficult to comprehend. Leading up to His arrest, Jesus had often spoken to the people in parables and figures of speech that the disciples struggled to understand, but at the end of John 16, His meaning starts to become clear. In fact, in verse 29, the disciples say, *"Ah, now you are speaking plainly and not using figurative speech!"* It's like they're finally able to understand Jesus for the first time, and it feels so good! Ironically, they *hear* Him, but they still don't quite understand. (And they didn't until His resurrection.)

Christ's message wasn't exactly good news, at least not from their perspective. In John 16: 31–33, Jesus says:

> *Do you now believe? Behold, the hour is coming, indeed it has come, when you will be scattered, each to his own home, and will leave me alone. Yet I am not alone, for the Father is with me. I have said these things to you, that in me you may have peace. In the world you will have tribulation. But take heart; I have overcome the world.*

SOMETHING TO THINK ABOUT

Jesus made it clear to the disciples that *He* was going to be their peace. He never told them peace was going to come from their circumstances, how nice their homes were, how many of their prayers He answered exactly the way they wanted, or whether they were physically and emotionally safe. No, after breaking the news that He was leaving and they would be scattered, He told them He would be their peace *in spite of* their circumstances—which would be troubled while they were living this side of heaven. Not exactly a peace-filled message.

When I was in my twenties, a friend of mine shared the details of his anger toward God, asking, "What has He ever done for me?" I'd only been walking closely with the Lord for a short time when we had that conversation, and I didn't know what to say then to help him. Now, twenty plus years later, I know he was looking for peace from the God he believed should want to give him a trouble-free life, not the God who gave up His only Son to give us eternal peace through salvation. My friend didn't understand that Jesus never promised to give us peace the way the world defines it. Instead, He promised His own arms to be a respite, a refuge in the storm, a place where we could run to get strength, comfort, and truth to see us through whatever troubled circumstances came our way. Jesus doesn't just give us peace; He *is* our peace. So if we want it, we have to run to Him.

EXTRA VERSES FOR STUDY OR PRAYER

John 14:27; Hebrews 12:14

VERSE OF THE DAY

I have said these things to you, that in me you may have peace. In the world you will have tribulation. But take heart; I have overcome the world.   —John 16:33

PRAYER

Father, thank You for making a way for us to have peace. When the world seeks to trouble us as it always will, we can find peace in who You are and what You did for us through Your Son. Help us learn to run to You. In Jesus's name, amen.

THINK

_____

_____

_____

PRAY

_____

_____

_____

PRAISE

———————————————————————————————
———————————————————————————————
———————————————————————————————

TO-DO

———————————————————
———————————————————
———————————————————

PRAYER LIST

———————————————————
———————————————————
———————————————————

QUESTIONS FOR DEEPER REFLECTION

1. Think about a recent time when your world felt out of control. What were your actual feelings or emotions during this time?

———————————————————————————————
———————————————————————————————

2. How did you fight through the fog of feeling overwhelmed to get back to some kind of normalcy? Did it work? Does anything need to change about your response?

———————————————————————————————
———————————————————————————————

Day 2

PEACE IS NOT AN EMOTION

READ GALATIANS 5

But the fruit of the Spirit is love, joy, peace, patience, kindness, goodness, faithfulness, gentleness, self-control; against such things there is no law.
—Galatians 5:22–23

Inside of the first prayer journal in this series, *Everyday Prayers for Joy*, my friend Gina Smith says, "The joy of the Lord is not an emotion. We experience it when we choose to focus on the grace God has poured out on us, the forgiveness He offers us, and the truths of His Word that keep us learning and growing."

I have read and reread the first sentence in this quote more times than I can count. "*The joy of the Lord is not an emotion.*" There's just something about it that causes me to stop and think; I can't help but ask, "If joy isn't an emotion, what is it? Isn't joy the way I feel when something goes my way? Isn't it what fills my heart to overflowing when my son makes a three-pointer, or gets a base hit? Isn't it the pride I feel when one of my children does their chores without being asked, holds the door for an elderly couple, or prays out loud at youth group?"

How is joy *not* an emotion? I mean, it's the way I *feel*.

You may be wondering why you're reading about the word *joy* in a prayer journal about *peace*. The answer is found in Galatians 5:22–23.

Paul is telling the early church at Galatia what they've learned about Christ and how to walk by the Spirit. Earlier, he had accused them of deserting the faith and *"turning to a different gospel"* (Galatians 1:6).

He reminds them that Christ has set them free from the *"yoke of slavery"* (Galatians 5:1) and invites them to do such wonderful things as love their neighbors as themselves (verse 14), be *"led by the Spirit"* (verse 18), and stay away from *"the works of the flesh"* (verses 19–21). Then, just after telling them all the things they need to flee from, he turns the tables and gives them a list of character traits that should be growing in their hearts and lives as they lay down the desires of the flesh and pick up learning and growing in their relationship with God—*"love, joy, peace, patience, kindness, goodness, faithfulness, gentleness, self-control"* (verses 22–23). See it there? Right beside the word *joy* is the word *peace*.

If joy is not an emotion, neither is peace. They're both fruit of the Spirit, fruit of a living, growing, life-altering relationship with Jesus. They aren't reactions to what's happening outside or around us; they're inward reflections of what God is growing in us. Fruit, not emotion. Response, not reaction. And by design, fruit grows as it's nurtured.

SOMETHING TO THINK ABOUT

When I read Gina's quote again through this new lens, I realize I've been trying to stuff a worldly definition of joy and peace into a biblical one. Round hole, square peg. It never really works, does it? To project the world's standards and definitions into the Bible? Shouldn't it be the other way around? To allow what the Bible says about everything influence how we understand the world? When we do this, we see that our peace comes not from our ability to control our circumstances—it isn't the absence of pain, struggle, or tribulation—but the growing presence of God in our lives. This presence crowds out chaos with the reminder of God's character as Provider, Protector, and Savior—loving, compassionate, generous, full of integrity, forgiving, good, holy, righteous, and so much more. What is missing from that list in order to have peace?

I can't find anything. In fact, every single circumstance or event that threatens to steal my peace is answered in the character of the living God and displayed through His Son, Jesus Christ. As I press into Him, I find it.

EXTRA VERSES FOR STUDY OR PRAYER

First Thessalonians 5:3; 2 Thessalonians 3:16

VERSE OF THE DAY

But the fruit of the Spirit is love, joy, peace, patience, kindness, goodness, faithfulness, gentleness, self-control; against such things there is no law. —Galatians 5:22–23

PRAYER

Father, no matter what happens today, help me find my peace in knowing Your character. Help me remember it in times of need and no matter what comes. May the response that comes from my heart reflect the work You continue to do in it. Help me find my peace in You. In Jesus's name, amen.

THINK

PRAY

PRAISE

_____

_____

_____

TO-DO

_____

_____

_____

PRAYER LIST

_____

_____

_____

QUESTIONS FOR DEEPER REFLECTION

1. What are the attributes or character traits of God that bring you peace? Make a list of them and keep it in your Bible.

_____

_____

2. What is your gut reaction or your first response to the idea that peace is not a feeling, but a fruit? Make it your prayer to ask God to grow this fruit in your life.

_____

_____

_____

Day 3

PEACE IS YOUR GIFT

READ JOHN 14

Peace I leave with you; my peace I give to you.
Not as the world gives do I give to you. Let not your hearts be
troubled, neither let them be afraid.
—John 14:27

Several years ago, my husband and I walked through a very painful set of circumstances. In fact, what we dealt with may just rank up there as one of the most painful things we've ever experienced to date. It deeply wounded us and caused us to question our callings, even who we were in Christ. Honestly, it caused us to question Christ Himself; we often found ourselves mad at God for allowing it to happen in the first place. We felt rejected, disrespected, and very, very alone.

Throughout the months that followed, we were confronted by this pain over and over, up and down, like waves of discouragement throughout the seasons. Sometimes things were fine…and then sometimes they were not. When things were fine, I was filled with hope, felt peaceful in my relationship with God and others, and went about my days feeling fulfilled in my Christian walk. When things were not fine, I was filled with fear, felt frustrated in my relationship with God and others, and went about my days wounded, wondering if I really had anything at all to offer the kingdom of God. It felt very much like being on a never-ending roller coaster of emotions, like having a bandage ripped off just as the wound started to heal, only to have to start the process all over again.

One day, as I saw the signs of an impending downward swing, I had an epiphany. As I was poised at the top of the roller-coaster tracks in that slow-motion moment just before the train takes a terrifying plunge, I felt like the Lord spoke to my heart.

He said, "Just get off."

Just get off. Choose not to take that ride anymore. Let's do something different.

That day, I wrote this in my own prayer journal: "No matter what happens in my life...regardless of whether this circumstance ever changes, ever heals...I have peace in my relationship with Jesus. *He is my peace.* I don't have to wait until the ride is over to get peace. I can choose to step off the ride and clasp the arm of the true Source of my peace right now. I'm choosing Him."

SOMETHING TO THINK ABOUT

John 14:27 specifically and clearly tells us that the kind of peace Jesus left us is not the same kind the world seeks to give us, and yet, so very often, I act like it should be. I could dwell on the longing of my heart to have peace in all my relationships, every circumstance, and with each new day, but that only means *I* want to control what happens to me, that I don't trust the God of the universe to give me the challenges I need to make me more like Him.

The other option is to choose the gift of peace Jesus died to give me. If I choose to look at Jesus as my peace, then anywhere I look, I see peace. Anywhere I go, I see peace. And any decision I make, I have peace.

Peace doesn't always come from what's happening in our lives, from our relationships, or even from making good decisions. We just aren't promised that kind of peace. But we *are* promised the peace Jesus gives. That kind of peace transcends any other and gives us the ability to release difficult relationships, circumstances, and even deep, deep wounds to the only One who can change them.

I invite you to step off the roller coaster of your own life and choose instead to walk with the gift of peace Jesus died to give you: Himself.

EXTRA VERSES FOR STUDY OR PRAYER

Psalm 122:6; Matthew 10:34

VERSE OF THE DAY

Peace I leave with you; my peace I give to you. Not as the world gives do I give to you. Let not your hearts be troubled, neither let them be afraid. —John 14:27

PRAYER

Father, thank You for healing our wounds more and more over time. Defend us and help us trust You with each circumstance we face. I pray and thank You that no weapon formed against us shall prosper. You are our Rock and Defender. I'm choosing to rest in that deep well of peace. I'm stepping off the roller coaster with Your help and praising You for making it possible. In Jesus's name, amen.

THINK

PRAY

PRAISE

_____

_____

_____

TO-DO

_____

_____

_____

PRAYER LIST

_____

_____

_____

QUESTIONS FOR DEEPER REFLECTION

1. Have you ever really thought about the fact that peace is a gift to you from God, not something you have to manufacture on your own in response to your circumstances?

_____

_____

_____

2. Where have you sought peace in the past? How has that worked for you?

_____

_____

_____

Day 4

HOW NOT TO BE ANXIOUS

READ PHILIPPIANS 4

Do not be anxious about anything, but in everything
by prayer and supplication with thanksgiving let your requests
be made known to God. And the peace of God,
which surpasses all understanding, will guard your hearts
and your minds in Christ Jesus.
—Philippians 4:6–7

I'm a firm believer that the Bible doesn't offer us a lot of formulas. For example, as the creator of Million Praying Moms, I talk a lot about being a praying mom and often share the story of how God used motherhood to kick my feet out from under me in all the best ways. I'm a very goal-oriented person, and until I became a mom, I had always been able to work hard enough to get the results I wanted. I naively thought the same would be true of parenting: hard work in, good kids out.

If you're a mom, you're laughing with me because you know this isn't necessarily true. If the Bible gave us a formula for raising good, godly kids, we'd all be doing it, and there would be fewer kids leaving the church when they turn eighteen. No, I learned the hard way that there's so much more to parenting than A + B = C.

But sometimes, the Bible does make us a promise.

I've experienced all kinds of different anxieties in my life. I'm sure you have too. If we could sit down together, we could probably make a list of all the different things there are to feel anxious about in the world…but the only thing we'd accomplish at the end is feeling more anxious.

Anxiety is generally defined as the absence of peace, and I'm willing to bet most Christians feel more anxious than peaceful. This is sad because, as we just discussed, Jesus died to give us peace—not the world's peace, but peace with Him, the kind of peace that transcends all others. So what can a Christian do when anxiety trumps peace? I believe there's a promise for us in Philippians 4:6–7 that will work every time, if we'll use it.

Go ahead and read this passage now and then ask yourself, "What if we actually lived like Philippians 4:6–7?"

SOMETHING TO THINK ABOUT

Read the passage carefully. Do you see them? In these verses, God gives us a step-by-step guide for peace in any circumstance—an active, living, life-altering, perspective-changing peace. Just follow along in this order:

1. When you feel anxious, catch yourself. You can even say, "Stop!" out loud as a message to yourself to interrupt your thought process and turn it in a new direction. Whatever you do, as soon as you recognize anxiety, stop it. Consider this the fulfillment of 2 Corinthians 10:4–5, which says, *"The weapons of our warfare are not of the flesh but have divine power to destroy strongholds. We destroy arguments and every lofty opinion raised against the knowledge of God, and take every thought captive to obey Christ."*

2. Go to God in prayer. Right away. Right now. Wherever you are. Need to go in the bathroom and hide? Do it. Need to pull over to the side of the road and bow your head? Do it. Need to get on your knees or maybe even on your face

before God in the bedroom where no one else can see? Get down. Don't let another moment pass without taking your anxieties and cares to God. Tell Him about them and ask Him to carry them for you.

3. Ask for peace. I promise, when you go through this process, you'll feel a sense of peace, sometimes right away. If you don't feel it right away, be like Jacob in Genesis 32:24–32 and wrestle with God in prayer until He blesses you with peace. Refuse to move from your prayer spot until He gives you peace and the ability to trust Him for the next step. And don't be afraid to do it again. The enemy wants you to be filled with anxiety because he knows it keeps you from functioning in the power of God. If you feel the anxiety creeping back in, go back to your prayer closet. Pull back over. Get back down on your knees. Keep taking it to God, and the victory will be yours. Your knees might hurt for a bit, but it'll be worth it.

4. Bonus step? Follow Philippians 4:8–9 and choose to focus your mind on whatever is true, honorable, just, pure, lovely, commendable, excellent, and worthy of praise. When you're filling your mind up with these things, there's not much room left for anxiety.

EXTRA VERSES FOR STUDY OR PRAYER
First Chronicles 22:9; Romans 15:13

VERSE OF THE DAY

Do not be anxious about anything, but in everything by prayer and supplication with thanksgiving let your requests be made known to God. And the peace of God, which surpasses all understanding, will guard your hearts and your minds in Christ Jesus.   —Philippians 4:6–7

PRAYER

Father, thank You for making a way, in all things, for us to live victoriously and peacefully in a world that lacks peace. In Jesus's name, amen.

THINK

_____

_____

_____

PRAY

_____

_____

_____

PRAISE

_____

_____

_____

TO-DO   PRAYER LIST

_____   _____

_____   _____

_____   _____

QUESTIONS FOR DEEPER REFLECTION

1. Are you an anxious person? Someone who feels things deeply in ways that affect your ability to function throughout the day?

_____

_____

_____

2. Make the connection that trust is the bridge between making your requests known to God and experiencing peace. Trust Him enough to go through the steps to peace He's outlined in His Word. Once you've given your feelings to God, trust that He's good and will take care of them. Do you trust Him?

_____

_____

_____

Day 5

BRING THE PEACE

READ MATTHEW 5

Blessed are the peacemakers:
for they shall be called the children of God.
—Matthew 5:9 (KJV)

When I'm on a plane ride, I like to sit in the aisle. I know that's weird, but I truly would rather not sit near the window if I can help it because I deal with motion sickness. Yes, the view from the window seat is spectacular, but you can't really enjoy it if your depth perception and churning stomach are threatening to make everyone around you miserable.

I've never actually lost my lunch on an airplane, but I've come pretty close a few times. It's the going up and the coming down that really get me. Once I'm in the air, I'm usually okay, but I don't like to take chances. As soon as I get on the plane, I put headphones on as a sign that I don't want to talk to anyone, reach for my trusty peppermint essential oil, and either start reading or listening to worship music. I *am* an introvert, but this ritual doesn't really have anything to do with my personality. It's all about trying to control my experience so I don't get sick and make everyone around me sick while I'm at it.

On one particular trip, heading to a speaking engagement at a women's event, I found myself not only fighting my usual motion sickness, but a sickness of the heart as well. I was nervous. Fearful. I wasn't a seasoned speaker, and I had left behind a bit of chaos for my husband to deal with. Not only that, but someone I cared about had recently questioned my motives for speaking and writing. I was shaken. Ironically—or perhaps not—as the plane ascended into the sky, a song I had forgotten I had downloaded came on. It's a song by Jason Gray called "With Every Act of Love."[2] The lyrics that caught my attention that day simply said, "With every act of love we bring the kingdom come."

SOMETHING TO THINK ABOUT

As believers in Jesus, we have the kingdom of God at work in us and through us...the Christ Himself, through the Holy Spirit, walking with us. With those lyrics ringing in my ears, I realized, perhaps for the first time—or maybe just in a new way—that I literally carried Jesus with me into every situation I encountered. Because of that, I had the ability to touch other people's lives with the kingdom through my own displays of love and kindness. Sounds a little bit like offering peace, doesn't it?

Matthew 5:9 is part of a larger discourse from Jesus called the Beatitudes. He's teaching the people what the kingdom of God actually looks like as it's lived out. Ironically, it doesn't look anything like they thought it would. Jesus gave the title "Blessed" to all kinds of things we wouldn't normally think of as blessed—things like being poor in spirit, meek, mourning, and hungering after righteousness. And there, in verse nine, He says, *"Blessed are the peacemakers."*

In his Bible commentary, the minister Matthew Henry wrote:

Such persons are blessed; for they have the satisfaction of enjoying themselves, by keeping the peace, and of being truly serviceable to others, by disposing them to peace. They are working together with Christ, who came into the world to slay all enmities, and to proclaim peace on earth. They shall be called the children of God...God will own them as such, and herein they will resemble him.

2. Jason Gray, "With Every Act of Love," on *Love Will Have the Final Word* (Centricity Music, 2014).

Was it possible that in seeing myself as a carrier of the kingdom (of sorts), I could actually start enjoying difficult situations by loving others and offering God's peace? Yes. Even if I felt shaken by my lack of expertise. Even when I felt offended and hurt by mean words. Even if I thought I was the least important person in the room and wondered if anyone even saw me.

I could still choose to be a part of what God is doing in the world by bringing His kingdom and offering peace.

EXTRA VERSES FOR STUDY OR PRAYER

Philippians 4:2; 2 Timothy 2:22

VERSE OF THE DAY

Blessed are the peacemakers: for they shall be called the children of God. —Matthew 5:9 (KJV)

PRAYER

Father, help me choose to bring Your peace into every situation I encounter. In Jesus's name, amen.

THINK

_____

_____

_____

PRAY

_____

_____

_____

PRAISE

_____

_____

_____

TO-DO   ## PRAYER LIST

_____   _____

_____   _____

_____   _____

QUESTIONS FOR DEEPER REFLECTION

1. When you enter a room, what mood do you bring with you? Peace? A storm? Kindness? Anger? Take a minute to think about what feeling other people associate with your presence.

_____

_____

_____

2. Is your answer to the first question what you *want* people to feel when they see you coming?

_____

_____

_____

Day 6

IN PURSUIT OF PEACE

READ 1 PETER 3

*Whoever desires to love life and see good days,
let him keep his tongue from evil and his lips from
speaking deceit; let him turn away from evil and do good;
let him seek peace and pursue it.*
—1 Peter 3:10–11

We were sitting in our home group when he said it. We'd just finished a luscious potluck spread, same as every Sunday after church, and had settled in to take prayer requests when our neighbor, a dear friend, shared how stressed out he was. His to-do list was just more than he could handle, his job was changing and might require a move, and, for goodness' sake, his yard needed to be mowed desperately, and he couldn't even find the time to do it.

Our neighbor didn't go directly home after our meeting that Sunday. His family had errands to run that kept them out for a few more hours. As my husband and I neared our house, we could see his tall grass—unusual for him—and we knew what we had to do. I honestly don't remember if I suggested it, or if it came from my husband's heart, but within a few moments of getting the boys out of the car and settled inside, he was out mowing our neighbor's yard…on a Sunday.

I don't know if people everywhere in the world are as picky about mowing on a Sunday as we are here in Virginia, but it's a big no-no where I'm from. In nearly twenty years of marriage, I can count on one hand the number of times my husband has done it, and all of them were either to help out someone else or because it was literally the only day he could get it done before we were living in a full-fledged jungle. I only had a twinge of guilt about it as I peeked outside to watch him serve someone we loved. We didn't own a riding lawn mower at the time, so he mowed their whole yard with a push mower.

We went to the window when we heard their car drive up. Our neighbor knew right away. He smiled, put his hand over his eyes like guys do when they don't want their wives to see their eyes have gotten a bit misty, and then he looked over our way. We just waved from the window and went on with our evening.

SOMETHING TO THINK ABOUT

First Peter 3:10–11 tells us to *"seek peace,"* but what does this actually mean? I think it can be directly related to another verse, Romans 12:18, which says, *"If possible, so far as it depends on you, live peaceably with all."*

That day—and many others like it that we experienced while we lived beside these particular neighbors—was an act of peace. This time, at least, we got it right. As much as it depended upon us, we pursued or lived at peace with those around us, just by doing something that was within our power to do. Mowing our neighbor's lawn wasn't a big deal to us, but it was to him.

Later that same year, Virginia suffered one of the largest snowstorms in recent history. Twenty-two inches of snow fell, which was actually over my youngest son's head at the time. My husband was out of commission, still on crutches after the first of two knee surgeries. The snow was falling quickly and accumulating faster than I could keep up with it. The boys tried to help out too, but they were still young, and it was exhausting work. A couple hours after our first attempt, I heard noises outside. When I opened the door to investigate, our neighbor looked up from shoveling our driveway, smiled at me, and said, "Love thy neighbor." He said the same thing to me each time he shoveled for us that evening while the snowstorm continued unabated. In fact, he not only kept our driveway mostly clear, he also dug a trench between our houses, so we could play cards over there. He carried my husband on his back, while I marched behind them, carrying the crutches.

Pursuing peace doesn't mean we have to be involved in treaties or conflict resolution, responding to chaos. I think pursuing peace simply means that God's people should be the ones acting in peace proactively, before they're asked, looking for ways to serve others so they can see Jesus living in and through us.

EXTRA VERSES FOR STUDY OR PRAYER

Psalm 34:14; Romans 12:17–18

VERSE OF THE DAY

Whoever desires to love life and see good days, let him keep his tongue from evil and his lips from speaking deceit; let him turn away from evil and do good; let him seek peace and pursue it.
—1 Peter 3:10–11

PRAYER

Father, help me see ways I can pursue peace proactively, so that I can better serve those You've given me to influence and show them what it looks like to follow Christ. In Jesus's name, amen.

THINK

PRAY

PRAISE

TO-DO

PRAYER LIST

QUESTIONS FOR DEEPER REFLECTION

1. Take a deep look at what comes out of your heart. Does it promote peace? Or something else?

---

2. If your answer to the first question fell a bit short (it did for me!) give God permission to show you the truth and make your heart more like His.

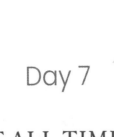

Day 7

AT ALL TIMES,
IN EVERY WAY

READ 2 THESSALONIANS 3

*Now may the Lord of peace himself give you peace at **all times** in **every way**. The Lord be with you all.*
—2 Thessalonians 3:16

Sometimes it's easier to find peace in the big, life-changing things than it is to find everyday peace. Painful emotions often come up again and again without warning and mess with the way we experience life. We don't ask for them, random things can trigger them, and most of us would prefer to slam the door in their face and call that peace. They often show up in the small parts of life—the cracks and crevices we thought we'd swept clean but somehow got dirty again.

As someone with a background in counseling, I know that denying difficult, peace-stealing feelings isn't necessarily the answer. Sometimes we need to allow ourselves to really *feel what we're feeling*, so to speak, so that our minds, hearts, and even physical bodies can heal. Most of the time, the feelings that return are ones that haven't been dealt with, or at least not completely.

And they can be sneaky.

After a particularly heated argument a few years ago, my oldest son looked at me and said, "Mom, I don't think you're really mad about what we've been arguing about. I think you're mad about something else, and our disagreement was just the icing on the cake." He was right. Something had caused me some pain earlier in the day, and I was still carrying it around later that night. Because I didn't recognize it for what it was, I allowed my emotions over a completely different issue to interfere with my relationship with my son.

I realize we're humans…emotional people…and I'm not trying to say that emotions are all bad. God did give them to us. I'm just saying that sometimes, our emotions hijack us completely and threaten to rob our peace. In fact, I would venture to guess that a high percentage of stress in our relationships and experiences throughout our days have little to do with the actual stressful events and more to do with the way our past experiences, or unhealed feelings related to those experiences, make us interpret them.

As believers, we can do something about this so that the offer God gives us in 2 Thessalonians 3:16 rings true. We really can have *"peace at all times in every way,"* and the best way to start is to simply ask God to show us when we're functioning from a place of hurt or frustration and not getting mad at our teenagers when they point it out. Realizing it is half the battle.

In my experience, God is gentle and compassionate. He only confronts us with what He knows we can handle together in that moment. Healing often takes place in layers, across time. The old phrase, "Time heals all wounds," really does have some truth to it, but there's even more power in that process for the Christian who knows what to do with unwanted emotions when they rear their ugly heads and try to steal our peace.

Like most people, I still deal with old hurts, but the difference between the Brooke you might see today versus the Brooke of ten years ago is that I know what to do with those wounds when they show up. My prayer for myself is that one day, I'll function from a place of peace instead of having to work to get there. The key to understanding this isn't to expect immediate victory. It's to know that kind of peace exists and be willing to work to live in it.

SOMETHING TO THINK ABOUT

Second Thessalonians 3:16 tells us two important pieces of information about peace.

1. God is the Lord of peace. He owns it. It's His.

2. He gives us *"peace at **all** times in **every** way."*

First, if peace belongs to God, that means He can give it the way He chooses. I sometimes wish God had chosen to do a lot of things differently, but I only wish that because I can't see the big picture, and I don't think the same way God does. If I did, I would probably agree with His methods. For now, I just have to trust them, and that means giving myself over to God's timetable for healing.

Second, God gives us *"peace at all times in every way."* What could this possibly mean, except exactly what it says? In my simple understanding, it literally means that no matter what happens to us, regardless of when unwanted emotions resurface and mess things up, God has made a way for us to have peace in that moment. Every time. In every way. Nothing excluded. But how?

By *taking, using,* and *growing* the gift of peace Jesus died to give us. It's already there. It's done. It's ours as believers in Jesus. He died, rose again, and is now seated at the right hand of God the Father. It is finished, so to speak. Peace is ours no matter what, but we have to choose to grab hold of it so we can overcome those pesky emotions we wish would go away.

Here's the deal: living a life filled with the gift of peace and every other gift that's ours in Christ takes intention. It takes choice and time; sometimes, it takes years to step into it fully. This may not be a process you master overnight. It might even be annoying to try it because it requires control and a desire to change. But it will be worth it. As you grow in peace, you'll see it.

EXTRA VERSES FOR STUDY OR PRAYER

Romans 15:13; Philippians 4:7

VERSE OF THE DAY

Now may the Lord of peace himself give you peace at all times in every way. The Lord be with you all. —2 Thessalonians 3:16

PRAYER

Father, You are my peace. You are the Lord of peace, and you've given me access to Your peace any time I need it. I need it, Lord. Give me the ability to choose peace over anything else because it glorifies You. In Jesus's name, amen.

THINK

PRAY

PRAISE

TO-DO

PRAYER LIST

_____

_____

_____

_____

_____

_____

QUESTIONS FOR DEEPER REFLECTION

1. When was the last time you asked God to give you peace
    in the morning? In the middle of the day? After dinner?
    When talking a walk? We tend to ask once and then quit,
    but it's important to remember that our God is peace, and
    He wants to be our peace at all times.

_____

_____

_____

2. If you had to explain to a new Christian what, "God is our
    peace," means, what would you say?

_____

_____

_____

_Note: Some traumatic experiences go beyond the scope of this
brief devotion, and while I do believe that God's Word speaks
to every form of emotional, physical, or spiritual hurt, if your
circumstance is more than just the everyday hurts most people
experience, I urge you to seek biblical counseling so you can get
the healing I know God wants you to have in Him. Much love
and prayers for your healing._   —Brooke

Day 8

SETTLE WHO'S IN CONTROL

READ PSALM 4

In peace I will both lie down and sleep; for you alone,
O LORD, make me dwell in safety.
—Psalm 4:8

I crouched in the corner of the room, sure that someone was going to attack me at any second. Literally squatting in the corner, hands over my head, all I could hear was the voice of the enemy saying, "You'll never win this. You're weak. You can't control it. God won't protect you."

As a child, I always struggled with fear of the dark. I slept with a night light well beyond the age at which most kids forgo them. In fact, I sometimes slept with all the lights on. I decided in college that scary movies weren't for me—I haven't watched one since 1996—but the fear of what might happen to me in the dark lingered well into my marriage.

On this particular occasion, someone had tried to break into the house where I was living alone, waiting for my husband to get a job transfer so we could buy our first house together. I had gone back the next day to gather my belongings and felt an immediate heaviness. Somehow, I gathered enough strength to walk in the door, but when I moved into the hallway, a door was closed that I knew I had left open…at least I really thought I had. When I saw it, I ran to the room I slept in and crouched down in the corner while fiery darts assailed me.

I don't know why I didn't run outside to my car and leave. Neither do I know for sure that someone had been there since I left the night before. What I do know is that my longtime fear of the dark came to a head that day, and I knew I had to make a choice.

Psalm 4:8 is one of a handful of verses that helped me make that choice, and I'm happy to report that now, twenty-some years later, I don't struggle with that same fear the way I used to. Sometimes it tries to step back up and bite, but mostly, I'm victorious over it. I've never crouched in the corner of a room allowing the voice of the enemy to beat me down again. He has no authority over me that I don't give him.

It's not that *I'm* necessarily in control, but I serve the One who is.

SOMETHING TO THINK ABOUT

The root of my personal issue with fear was a lack of trust in the goodness of God. I thought the only way God could be good was if He kept me safe. As a part of my healing, I had to ask myself if I would still think God was good even if my worst fears came true. It took a long time to get to the answer, but when I did, I was free. During that time, I memorized and quoted Psalm 4:8 over and over. I had it framed beside my bed so it was the last thing I saw at night when the lights went out. It was written on sticky notes and posted strategically around my apartment, and it was what my mind worked through and tried desperately to believe as I fell asleep.

The truth was that I could lock the doors, pull down the shades, turn on an alarm, or even create a barricade to my room, which I did once, but nothing could prevent evil from finding me. I found strength in believing and praying the truth: God alone gave me protection, and nothing could come to me that didn't first go through Him. I reflected on the story of Job in the Old Testament—horrible though it was—and knew God needed me to understand this important truth. Only then could I have peace.

Freedom from fear and knowing how to get free from fear has served me well beyond my issues with darkness. It translates easily to fear of man, fear of financial failure, fear of the cost of obedience, fear of losing my children, and any other kind of fear you can name. The answer is never what I can do to keep myself safe; it's always trusting God to keep me safe within His will.

EXTRA VERSES FOR STUDY OR PRAYER

Isaiah 26:3; Romans 12:18

VERSE OF THE DAY

In peace I will both lie down and sleep; for you alone, O Lord, make me dwell in safety.   —Psalm 4:8

PRAYER

Father, You alone keep me and my family safe. No amount of outside protection can protect me better than You. Make me and those I love dwell in safety. In Jesus's name, amen.

THINK

_____

_____

_____

PRAY

_____

_____

_____

PRAISE

_____

_____

_____

TO-DO

_____

_____

_____

PRAYER LIST

_____

_____

_____

QUESTIONS FOR DEEPER REFLECTION

1. Have you ever been afraid of the dark? Do you have a child who's afraid to be alone at night? Reflect for a moment on what this sensation feels like and how you've fought it in the past.

_____

_____

_____

2. The only thing that overcomes fear is absolute trust in the goodness of God. What more could we ask for to give us peace?

_____

_____

_____

Day 9

HAVE A STAYED MIND

READ ISAIAH 26

You keep him in perfect peace whose mind is stayed on you,
because he trusts in you.
—Isaiah 26:3

Did you skip Day 8 for some reason? I hope not because its message lays the groundwork nicely for today's devotion. If you haven't read it yet, go back and take care of it. It's important because repeating the truths of Scripture to myself over and over again, while lying in bed afraid, was my first real attempt at having a *stayed* mind.

I had grown up listening to an old hymn that includes this refrain:

Turn your eyes upon Jesus,
Look full in His wonderful face,
And the things of earth will grow strangely dim,
In the light of His glory and grace.[3]

I knew the words by heart, but I'd never had the chance to prove them until the day after someone broke into the house where I was living. (Seriously, if you skipped Day 8, go back!) In His kindness, God allowed me to see the consequences of taking my eyes off of Him.

In Matthew 14:24–32, the disciples were in one of their boats far from land, and Jesus came to them, walking on the churning, roiling

---

3. Helen Howarth Lemmel, "The Heavenly Vision," *Glad Songs* (London: National Sunday School Union, 1922).

waters of the Sea of Galilee. After Jesus assured them that He was not a ghost, Peter said, *"Lord, if it is you, command me to come to you on the water"* (verse 28). Jesus bid him to step out of the boat, and Peter *"walked on the water and came to Jesus"* (verse 29). But then he took his eyes off the Master. Noticing the wind and the waves, Peter began to sink.

Peter's first steps were full of confidence and trust, but then he began to notice what was happening all around him. Like many of us, Peter took his eyes off of Jesus and turned them to the things of this world. Instantly, he was afraid; lacking trust, he lost his peace.

For me, the process of overcoming my fears was one of trusting God to be good no matter what was happening in my life. Doesn't that just mirror Isaiah 26:3 perfectly? The reason we can have perfect peace as we look at Jesus, keeping our minds *"stayed"* on Him, is because we see clearly how trustworthy He really is.

SOMETHING TO THINK ABOUT

Having a mind *"stayed"* on our Savior simply means controlling our thoughts and attention so we're focused on the truth—God's character, His care for us, and His forgiveness, love, compassion, and provision—instead of being focused on our circumstances. *Turn your eyes upon Jesus, look full in His wonderful face.* I once heard a pastor say, "Glance at your problems. Gaze at Jesus." He was 100 percent correct.

Jesus made it clear what would happen after He ascended into heaven. We will have troubles while we're on this earth. (See John 16:33.) It's a promise. Our circumstances will seemingly careen out of control, our kids will sin, our friends will abandon us, and our best-laid plans will crumble to pieces. Moreover, we'll be persecuted for following Jesus. It isn't supposed to be easy. But with our minds focused on Jesus, while acknowledging the problems in life, we can choose to believe what God says over what we can see.

Finances in ruin? God can make a way.

Children turned from the faith? God can make a way.

Marriage struggling? God can make a way.

Relationships broken? God specializes in taking the broken and making it beautiful.

He's the Redeemer, the Provider, the Sustainer, the Healer, the Forgiver, the Lover, the Giver—I could go on and on. When you spend your time intentionally thinking about the great goodness of God, what's left to worry about?

EXTRA VERSES FOR STUDY OR PRAYER

Exodus 14:14; Psalm 122:7

VERSE OF THE DAY

You keep him in perfect peace whose mind is stayed on you, because he trusts in you.   —Isaiah 26:3

PRAYER

Father, there are so many things vying for my attention. Good things. Worthy things. Big things. Scary things. Things I have to do. Things I'd like to avoid. Somehow, in the midst of it all, help me keep my mind set on You. In Jesus's name, amen.

THINK

_____

_____

_____

PRAY

_____

_____

_____

PRAISE

_____

_____

_____

TO-DO   PRAYER LIST

_____   _____

_____   _____

_____   _____

QUESTIONS FOR DEEPER REFLECTION

1. Make a list of all the things that pull your eyes away from
    Jesus. It could be bills, issues with your children, serious
    relationship issues, work, or health problems. Or, it could
    just be distractions, like sports, television shows, social
    media, or chores.

_____

_____

_____

2. Now make a second list. For each item on the first list, write
    a character trait of God that makes you feel like it will be
    taken care of, or that is better than the worst distraction.

_____

_____

_____

Day 10

LET PEACE RULE

READ COLOSSIANS 3

And let the peace of Christ rule in your hearts,
to which indeed you were called in one body. And be thankful.
—Colossians 3:15

The summer my son played in 13U, a youth travel baseball league, he struggled with pitching. In the fall of that same year, the beginning of the travel season, he'd received an award from his coach for being one of the best, most consistent pitchers on the team. His proud mama had even posted on social media the first time he threw a shutout…and maybe, just maybe, was a little bit obnoxious in her pride and excitement for him.

But something happened between the fall and the spring.

Throughout their progression in age, baseball players know that the size of the field and the distance between bases gets bigger and longer, until they reach the same size field the big leaguers play on: ninety feet between each base and sixty feet six inches from the pitcher's mound to home plate. During the fall of the 13U year, pitchers transition from a fifty-foot distance to fifty-four feet and stay there until the spring. Then, the mound moves back another six feet and stays at sixty feet six inches until they stop playing baseball. Playing a few months at fifty-four feet is supposed to help ease the pretty major jump to sixty feet and give pitchers time to strengthen their arm and grow. At fifty-four feet, my son was owning the mound. At sixty, he fell apart.

After a few tournaments in which it was clear my guy was going to struggle to even throw a strike, I took him in for an emergency session with his pitching coach. I said, "Drew, he's broken. Fix him." Drew watched my son throw a few times from a mound at his facility and then proceeded to break down exactly what my son was doing wrong.

My sons are late bloomers. Even though they were both almost nine pounds when they were born, it took them a long time to catch up to their peers in growth after the age of about ten. So while most of the other pitchers grew between the fall and spring of their 13U year, my son had not. And to compensate for the extra six feet of distance he had to throw the ball, he was pushing from the wrong place in his body, mustering all the strength he had to get the ball across home plate with any kind of speed. It sounds like that would work, but in reality, he was letting bad mechanics rule his delivery of the ball, causing his pitch to be off enough that he was throwing consistent balls instead of consistent strikes.

Drew took the ball from my son's hand, placed his body in the proper stance, and showed him how to move it to get the most power. Then he said something I will never forget: "Now, just let the ball go across home plate."

Just let it.

SOMETHING TO THINK ABOUT

Colossians 3:15 says, *"And **let** the peace of Christ rule in your hearts."* The word *"let"* in this verse confirms to me that the peace of Christ is ours for the taking if we're followers of Jesus. God has already made it available. We just have to let it do the work in our hearts. With Drew as his guide, my son had all the tools he needed to "let the ball go across home plate" in the right spot to throw a strike.

God, as our Guide, has made His peace available to us through the person of His Son. Our job is to let that peace rule in our hearts in place of other things designed to steal it. We might need correction.

Sometimes, we'll be tempted to muster up peace the wrong way and position ourselves poorly, but the peace God offers never goes away. It will always give us exactly what we need to get through this life.

If we let it.

EXTRA VERSES FOR STUDY OR PRAYER

Romans 8:6; Romans 12:18

VERSE OF THE DAY

And let the peace of Christ rule in your hearts, to which indeed you were called in one body. And be thankful.
—Colossians 3:15

PRAYER

Father, thank You for all the things You have already provided for those who are called according to Your name. So much is available to us that we don't take. Help us see Your gifts and make them ours. Let them rule in our hearts and give us peace. In Jesus's name, amen.

THINK

_____

_____

_____

PRAY

_____

_____

_____

PRAISE

_____

_____

_____

TO-DO   PRAYER LIST

_____   _____

_____   _____

_____   _____

QUESTIONS FOR DEEPER REFLECTION

1. Have you ever considered the idea that you're not taking advantage of certain gifts, like peace, that God has made available to you?

_____

_____

_____

2. Get practical. Pick one difficult circumstance you encountered over the past week and describe what it might've looked like to *"let the peace of Christ rule"* in your heart instead of what actually did rule there.

_____

_____

_____

Day 11

FILLED TO OVERFLOWING

READ JUDE 1

*To those who are called, beloved in God the Father
and **kept** for Jesus Christ: May mercy, peace,
and love be multiplied to you.*
—Jude 1:1–2

The letter of Jude is a short call-to-action for believers in Christ. It's so short that it often gets overlooked entirely. I honestly can't remember ever hearing an expository sermon on the book of Jude or listening to a preacher teach all the way through it, verse by verse. I've heard bits and pieces woven into larger sermons as supporting verses, but never anything on the book as a whole. So as I was preparing to write to you about the first two verses, I decided to reread and study the whole thing.

The entire book is a little over six hundred words and takes up one page in my Bible. Not front and back, just the front. It's short and sweet, but packed with useful, important information for the believer. I highly recommend reading the whole thing and studying it today if you have the time. For this devotional today, we're going to camp in verses one and two—and mainly on one word, "*kept*," or, as the King James Version has it, "*preserved.*"

To preserve something means to safeguard, look after, protect, or maintain. One of the most common arguments we have in our home occurs when our two teenage boys can't find the equipment they need for a baseball tournament. Baseball requires a lot of individual parts and pieces, including gloves, bats, cleats, cups, hats, uniform socks, compression shirts, sliding pants, and the right combination of uniform pants and shirts. If you happen to be a catcher, add another five or so pieces of equipment to that list. (Thankfully, my kids are not catchers!)

For years, my husband has tried to help our boys learn to keep everything in the same place so they'll always know where it is. We even set aside time on Friday nights, before a Saturday tournament, to gather all the necessary items and lay them out on the kitchen table. And yet, almost every *very* early Saturday morning, we're missing something. There's nothing worse than getting up before dawn on a Saturday and running around like crazy people, looking for a missing cup, instead of sleeping in. Just sayin'. That part of the body has to be protected if I want grandchildren someday, so we're not leaving the house without it.

We try hard to teach our children to keep, maintain, and take care of the things they need and care about—even if those things can usually be found in a dark corner, or under their bed—but our efforts fall short most weekends.

Not so with God.

SOMETHING TO THINK ABOUT

According to *The Wiersbe Bible Commentary*, to keep or preserve means to carefully watch and guard something. So these verses from Jude tell us that not only are we set apart for God's purposes, called by the gospel to trust in Jesus for salvation, and loved by the Father, we are also *kept* by God for His own glory. As Warren W. Wiersbe wrote, "He is able to preserve us in our daily walk and keep us from stumbling."[4]

I don't know about you, but I'm more like my kids than I'd like to admit, especially to them. I stumble so often and need to be preserved. The knowledge that God can, and will, do this in spite of my

4. Warren W. Wiersbe, *The Wiersbe Bible Commentary* (Colorado Springs, CO: David C. Cook, 2007), 1023.

own inability and weakness fills me with hope and comfort. And it's because we are God's children—called, beloved, and kept—that we are the recipients of His mercy, peace, and love, not just once at the point of salvation but for always. We can count on being kept and receiving mercy, peace, and love because God can be counted on to glorify Himself.

EXTRA VERSES FOR STUDY OR PRAYER

Second Corinthians 13:11; 1 Thessalonians 5:13

VERSE OF THE DAY

To those who are called, beloved in God the Father and kept for Jesus Christ: May mercy, peace, and love be multiplied to you.
—Jude 1:1–2

PRAYER

Father, thank You for keeping me. Left to myself I know I would never be able to stay. There's too much sin still in my heart, and it's prone to wander from You. The knowledge that You will preserve me, that You will guard me and keep me from stumbling, brings me peace. In Jesus's name, amen.

THINK

PRAY

PRAISE

TO-DO

PRAYER LIST

QUESTIONS FOR DEEPER REFLECTION

1. Define the words *mercy*, *peace*, and *love* by biblical standards. Use a Bible dictionary if you need to.

2. How does it make you feel to know that God is committed to keeping you and your family because doing so brings glory to Him?

3. Will God ever not glorify Himself?

Day 12

REAPING AND SOWING

READ JAMES 3

And a harvest of righteousness is sown
in peace by those who make peace.
—James 3:18

A dear friend of mine is estranged from her family. Every year at Christmastime, she sends an invitation for them to come to her house to celebrate…and every year, they don't show up. Christmas is a time of peace. It's written everywhere. From signs on the road to songs on the radio, "Peace on earth" slogans abound and cause us to hope for something we haven't quite found yet. So it is with my friend. If ever there was a time to hope for peace in her family, it's at Christmas. So she invites, and they don't come.

I asked her once why she keeps asking, keeps inviting, and her answer reminded me of the reaping and sowing principle we see throughout Scripture. What you put in, you get back out…generally. In her case, making peace available to her family, even when she knows they may not take it, is her part of the job. Her door is open, and the offer of peace is on the table. She sows and hopes that one day, she'll reap. Maybe it'll be next Christmas, and maybe it won't. Maybe each year she's planting a seed of peace that will grow until her family's hearts are open to reconciliation and forgiveness. That's what she's praying for, but if it never happens, she can rest in knowing that she's sown in faith and tended in prayer. The rest is up to God.

Real wisdom, God's wisdom, begins with a holy life and is characterized by getting along with others. It is gentle and reasonable, overflowing with mercy and blessings, not hot one day and cold the next, not two-faced. You can develop a healthy, robust community that lives right with God and enjoy its results only if you do the hard work of getting along with each other, treating each other with dignity and honor. —James 3:17–18 MSG

The truth is, there will be people we can't get along with—at least not for more time than it takes to have Christmas dinner—but that doesn't mean we don't invite them over for Christmas dinner and plant a seed of peace. There will be relationships in our lives that bear fruit only if we do the hard work of getting along, at least attempting to treat each other *"with dignity and honor."* That's the way it is because we're sinners. There will be hurts that make us want to hurt back, but God's Word is clear that we're to *make* peace instead. What does this mean?

SOMETHING TO THINK ABOUT

We have a large garden at the back of our property in rural Southwest Virginia. Every spring and summer, my husband and his dad work themselves silly to prepare the earth, soften the earth, plant the seeds, tend the seeds, protect the seeds, and then, Lord willing, harvest the fruit of their labor. They spend hours and hours each year creating something special that everyone in our community comments on.

My father-in-law is the mastermind of this endeavor, possessing a lifetime of firsthand experience with making things grow. My husband is learning. He's the grunt labor guy for now, but over time, he has picked up on lessons from his father and will continue to do so until he plants a garden on his own. But without that grunt labor, without the knowledge of the land and the hours of sweat equity they both put in, there would be no fruit.

What we put in, we get out. It's simple in concept, but rarely easy in practice. But even if it takes our whole lives, it's worth the effort when we get to taste the goodness of God in what's produced.

EXTRA VERSES FOR STUDY OR PRAYER

Isaiah 54:13; Mark 9:50

VERSE OF THE DAY

And a harvest of righteousness is sown in peace by those who make peace.   —James 3:18

PRAYER

Father, give us the desire to do the right thing, even if the favor isn't returned, sowing seeds of peace in the dark, troubled places of our lives. Over time, Lord, we pray that You will grow those seeds, produce fruit that glorifies Your name, and produce a harvest of righteousness in Your people. In Jesus's name, amen.

THINK

_____

_____

_____

PRAY

_____

_____

_____

PRAISE

_____

_____

_____

TO-DO

_____

_____

_____

PRAYER LIST

_____

_____

_____

QUESTIONS FOR DEEPER REFLECTION

1. Think back to your answers to the reflection questions for Day 5. _Do_ you bring the peace of God with you wherever you go? How could you do this more? What would need to change?

_____

_____

_____

2. What's one way you could make or sow peace in a troubled area of your life today?

_____

_____

_____

Day 13

DON'T BE
A LINE DANCER

READ PSALM 34

Turn away from evil and do good; seek peace and pursue it.
—Psalm 34:14

Sometimes, as Christians, we ask the wrong questions. When I was growing up, in the thick of the purity movement, teenagers and young adults often asked, "How far is too far?" I think they genuinely wanted to know where the line was, so as not to offend God, but that question also revealed a deeper misunderstanding of what God's Word says about sin.

Imagine with me a line drawn in the sand. In a weird game on the beach, you're asked to dance as close to the line as you possibly can without going over. If you can do it, you win the prize—and you really want that prize—so you start dancing. The music starts, and in the beginning, your gaze is focused hard on that line. As your feet move in time to the music, the line is all you can see. Your mind chants with the beat of the song, "Don't step over the line. Don't step over the line."

But then something changes. Slowly, as you dance longer and harder, your resolve starts to weaken, and the line starts to blur. Your steps widen and become more carefree. Before you know what's happened, you accidentally step over the line. Game over. Prize lost.

Psalm 34:14 gives us an entirely different way of looking at the question of the line. It doesn't tell us to dance as close to the line of sin as we can without going over. It doesn't say dance with evil and try not to get burned. It says, *"Turn away from evil and do good."* Turn around with your back to the line and run as fast and as far away from it as you can. Flee in the opposite direction.

"How far is too far?" is the wrong question. The right question might be, "Where do You want me to go, Lord?"

And it's not just about purity. This insight gets wrongly applied to any sin we're grappling with. As long as we keep dancing as close as possible to the line, trying not to step over it, we won't have peace.

SOMETHING TO THINK ABOUT

When I was in my twenties, I was trying to overcome a particular sin and failing over and over. I remember thinking and praying a lot about this process, until finally, I had to admit that I *wanted* to sin. That was the real problem. I kept putting myself in a situation where I had to face this sin because I *wanted* to. More than that, I *loved* my sin. I was running toward it, feeling guilty for dancing so close to the line that I stepped over it.

I don't remember what verse or passage I was studying when this realization hit me, but I do remember that I was sitting on my bed at my parents' house when God showed me that the only way I could overcome this sin—any sin, really—was to love Jesus more than I loved anything else. And that, my friend, is what it looks like to turn in the opposite direction and run the other way. I repented right there on my childhood bed and took the first steps away from the line and into the arms of Jesus. I won't say everything was perfect from then on, but as I learned to love Jesus, my desire for what God calls evil diminished.

There is no peace to be found in the pursuit of evil or even in dancing around it. Seeking peace, pursuing peace, means running toward Christ, knowing Him better and loving Him more than anything else.

He's the prize.

EXTRA VERSES FOR STUDY OR PRAYER

Ephesians 4:3; Colossians 3:15

VERSE OF THE DAY

Turn away from evil and do good; seek peace and pursue it.
—Psalm 34:14

PRAYER

Father, give us eyes to see the evil in our lives. Give us the ability and desire to turn away from evil and toward You, our peace. In Jesus's name, amen.

THINK

PRAY

PRAISE

TO-DO

PRAYER LIST

QUESTIONS FOR DEEPER REFLECTION

1. What do you think it means to *pursue* peace?

    ---

2. Read the story of Cain and Abel in Genesis 4:1–7. What do you think it means that sin was *crouching* at Cain's door? Does it crouch at yours? According to Genesis 4:7, what must you do about it?

Day 14

AS MUCH AS
IT DEPENDS ON YOU

READ HEBREWS 12:14

Strive for peace with everyone, and for the holiness without which no one will see the Lord.
—Hebrews 12:14

After reading Hebrews 12:14, I prayed, "Really, Lord? Even after all this time?"

When I was in my early twenties, I had a falling out with a friend I loved dearly. Things were said and done that were difficult to come back from…hard to take back. We were both in the wrong. Personally, I know that my wrong came from the way I responded to her wrong, but regardless, there was sin on both sides, and a friendship that had spanned a lifetime fell apart. Now, about five years later, I sat behind my computer screen, knowing I had to reach out.

Would she respond?

Would she even talk to me?

Would she even read my email?

She did all of the above. However, she basically said there was no reason for us to continue our friendship. By that time, we lived thousands of miles apart, and while she appreciated my email and apology for my part in our broken fellowship, she didn't see the point of staying in contact.

It hadn't been an easy email for me to write, and her email in return certainly wasn't easy to read. I wish it had gone differently. I wish we'd had more time to talk through what happened so we could reconcile and heal, but one extended hand doesn't a handshake make. I didn't receive an invitation to her wedding, even though it was local, and have only spoken to her on Facebook a time or two in the last twenty years. You'd think that twenty years would be enough to erase some of the hurt and the shame I feel over my own actions, but it isn't. I still wish we could reconcile. Fully. But that may never happen.

SOMETHING TO THINK ABOUT

One of the main frustrations over this is that I want to fix it, but I can't. Don't get me wrong—I don't think about it every day or even every month. But when I do think about this friend I've lost, I lament the fact that I can't make it better on my own. Some things in life are just like that. Thankfully, Scripture speaks to this issue and gives us comfort when we face it.

Here's a complementary verse to the one for today:

*If possible, **so far as it depends on you**, live peaceably with all.*
—Romans 12:18

When I felt convicted to reach out to my old friend and ask for forgiveness, I was striving to be at peace with her as much as it depended upon me. The problem is that peace doesn't always just depend upon me. Despite this, I can have *personal* peace in knowing I've done everything I can.

The rest is up to God.

EXTRA VERSES FOR STUDY OR PRAYER

Isaiah 48:22; 2 Peter 1:2

VERSE OF THE DAY

Strive for peace with everyone, and for the holiness without which no one will see the Lord. —Hebrews 12:14

PRAYER

Father, thank You for the peace that comes in knowing we followed Your example, even if things didn't turn out perfectly. Please continue to work in our hearts and relationships to bring healing and reconciliation. In Jesus's name, amen.

THINK

_____

_____

_____

PRAY

_____

_____

_____

PRAISE

_____

_____

_____

TO-DO

_____

_____

_____

PRAYER LIST

_____

_____

_____

QUESTIONS FOR DEEPER REFLECTION

1. What is one small step you can take to be at peace with someone you've not been at peace with in the past?

_____

_____

_____

2. Even if there's nothing more we can physically do to make peace with someone, we can still pray for them and pray for God to move in the situation. Do that now with an area of your life that lacks peace.

_____

_____

_____

Day 15

HOW TO RECOGNIZE GOD'S WISDOM

READ JAMES 3

*But the wisdom from above is first pure, then peaceable,
gentle, open to reason, full of mercy and good fruits,
impartial and sincere.*
—James 3:17

If I've asked God once for wisdom, I've asked a thousand times. More than once, I've wished for writing on the wall or an audible voice telling me what to do. In my heart, I want to obey God. I want to go where He leads. I want to make decisions that reflect Him well to the people around me, and I want to do things His way. So, I ask for wisdom. But more than once, I've struggled to recognize God's wisdom when it came, questioning if I was hearing correctly, or if what I heard was really God at all.

Am I listening to my own heart? The Bible says it's *"deceitful above all things"* (Jeremiah 17:9). Or is this leaning I feel really the hand of God moving in my life? How do I know the difference? Will I always be able to *know* really and truly that how I'm feeling is a leading from God? Sometimes it's hard to tell the difference.

Once, I worked for a man who had moved to Virginia from Michigan. Beforehand, he had applied for several jobs in the same field and received invitations from two different ministries, in two different states, at the same time, for exactly the same position. As he and his wife prayed about which job to take, they both felt a peace about *both* jobs. He actually told me that they believed the Lord had opened the door to either, and they were free to go wherever they wanted.

I have to tell you, friends, this blew my twenty-something mind wide open! I had literally never experienced anything like that before—and frankly, I didn't like it. I don't want God to give me options! I want Him to tell me what to do so I can do it.

You might have guessed that I have some control issues. Yes, it's true. Disguised behind my sincere desire to do God's will is an equally sincere desire to feel like I know where I'm going and how I'm going to get there. I don't like unknowns.

Unfortunately, this desire of mine isn't supported by Scripture. God told Abraham to leave home and family, and *"go out to a place that he was to receive as an inheritance. And he went out, not knowing where he was going. By faith he went to live in the land of promise"* (Hebrews 11:8–9; also see Genesis 12:1–5).

"Not knowing where he was going…"

I don't know how you feel about those six words, but they scare me to death. I'm a very goal-oriented person. When I was in high school, my dad and I regularly had *success conversations*. We talked about my goals and the stepping stones I needed to walk across to reach them. When I was eighteen, I knew exactly where I was going and what needed to happen to get me there. Of course, life turned out differently than I expected, and there were surprises, twists, and turns along the way. Sometimes, it really is hard to know what's God's wisdom and what's our own, but I've found that James 3:17 helps.

SOMETHING TO THINK ABOUT

Wiersbe wrote:

Worldly wisdom will produce worldly results; spiritual wisdom will give spiritual results. Worldly wisdom produces trouble…Wrong thinking produces wrong living. One reason the world is in such a mess is because men have refused to accept the wisdom of God.[5]

These days, as a forty-something mom of two teenage boys, I find myself asking less for wisdom about big life goals and more for wisdom in how to deal with what life is presenting our family with in the moment. I recognize that I don't possess all the wisdom I need to be the kind of mom I want to be, and this knowledge of my lack of control makes me cry out to God for *His* wisdom. In truth, I need all the wisdom I can get. I fall woefully short in so many ways; left to myself, I'm bound to make mistakes. Thankfully, His Word says He'll give us wisdom when we ask in faith. (See James 1:5–6.)

Scripture also helps me understand what to look for in order to recognize God's wisdom. If what I feel God leading me to do or say is pure, peaceable, gentle, open to reason, full of mercy and good fruits, impartial and sincere, I can be pretty sure it's God. If it lacks these things, it's probably not.

Next time you find yourself trying to discern if something is the wisdom of God or the wisdom of man, measure it against James 3:17. Align your thinking with God's thinking and be assured that there will be good fruit, even if it doesn't happen right away. Then, make a choice, walking boldly in the knowledge that as you have tried to honor Him, the outcome rests with the Lord.

EXTRA VERSES FOR STUDY OR PRAYER

Romans 5:1; Ephesians 2:14

VERSE OF THE DAY

But the wisdom from above is first pure, then peaceable, gentle, open to reason, full of mercy and good fruits, impartial and sincere. —James 3:17

---

5. Wiersbe, *The Wiersbe Bible Commentary*, 873.

PRAYER

Father, thank You for being true and trustworthy and for giving us the tools we need to follow You. When we need wisdom, help us remember to ask You for it, and give us the desire and ability to measure all things against Your Word, our standard. In Jesus's name, amen.

THINK

PRAY

PRAISE

TO-DO

PRAYER LIST

QUESTIONS FOR DEEPER REFLECTION

1. How would you describe the difference between the wisdom that comes from God and wisdom that comes from the world?

_____

_____

_____

2. Is there a situation right now in your life where you could use God's wisdom? Try measuring it against James 3:17 and write about what God shows you.

_____

_____

_____

Day 16

LEARNING NOT TO
BE CLUMSY

READ PSALM 119:165

*Great peace have those who love your law;
nothing can make them stumble.*
—Psalm 119:165

Psalm 119 is the longest of the Psalms, and it's the perfect point of focus for the mind of all believers. We don't know for sure who wrote it or when it was written, but in all but a few short verses, the psalmist speaks directly to God as if he's in a loving relationship that will endure through almost anything, even persecution. The psalmist clearly has a deep and abiding love of the Word of God, placing high value on keeping it.

In the 176 verses of Psalm 119, we're told that the Word of God keeps our ways pure (v. 9), keeps us from sinning (v. 11), brings us delight (v. 24), strengthens us (v. 28), gives us comfort in affliction (v. 50), teaches us good judgment and gives us knowledge (v. 66), gives us life (v. 93), makes us wise (v. 98), provides us with understanding (v. 104), gives light to our paths (v. 105), fills us with joy (v. 111), gives us a hiding place and shield (v. 114), imparts understanding to the simple (v. 130), and gives us peace (v. 165).

With all of these glorious benefits of the Word of God at work in our lives, is it any wonder that those who love it have peace and protection against stumbling?

SOMETHING TO THINK ABOUT

I've often thought that the verses surrounding today's highlighted verse (161–168) are perfect for a morning affirmation or a prayer to start the day:

> *Princes persecute me without cause, but my heart stands in awe of your words. I rejoice at your word like one who finds great spoil. I hate and abhor falsehood, but I love your law. Seven times a day I praise you for your righteous rules. Great peace have those who love your law; nothing can make them stumble. I hope for your salvation, O LORD, and I do your commandments. My soul keeps your testimonies; I love them exceedingly. I keep your precepts and testimonies, for all my ways are before you.*

Truly, our author loves the Lord and wants to walk in His ways. But what does it mean to love God's law?

In this psalm, the author uses the word *"law"* to mean the Torah or the first five books of the Old Testament. The books of the Torah tell the story of how God created the world, the birth of mankind and its fall, the choosing of God's people, their slavery in Egypt, the exodus from Egypt into the wilderness, and the death of Moses just before his people go into the promised land. It was likely that this is all the author of this psalm had access to as *holy Scriptures*. It's interesting that what so many Christians today think of as the *boring* part of the Bible, this man loved with all his being. It was all of God that he had, so he loved it. Studied it. Memorized it. Prayed it. Allowed it to dictate and direct his life and choices. Gave it permission to correct his thoughts. Used it to define everything else.

When revered this way, the Word of God seeps into the heart of sinful mankind and becomes the lens through which they see everything else. Yesterday, we learned that wrong thinking produces wrong living. In contrast, right thinking—supported by God's right, true Word—produces right living. And when we think right, we act right. When we act right, we stumble less. And when we don't fear stumbling, we have more peace.

EXTRA VERSES FOR STUDY OR PRAYER

Romans 14:17; 1 Timothy 2:2

VERSE OF THE DAY

Great peace have those who love your law; nothing can make them stumble. —Psalm 119:165

PRAYER

Father, may these words be our truth. May they define our days and the moments of our days. May our children walk also in Your ways, loving Your Word, and keeping Your law. In Jesus's name, amen.

THINK

_____

_____

_____

PRAY

_____

_____

_____

PRAISE

TO-DO

_____

_____

_____

PRAYER LIST

_____

_____

_____

QUESTIONS FOR DEEPER REFLECTION

1. How would you rate your commitment to and understanding of God's truth found in His Word? Do you love it?

---

2. Difficult seasons of life tend to show us exactly how much we love God and His Word. When was the last time you went through something hard? Were you able to stand on what you knew to be true of God's Word? Did you stumble? Why?

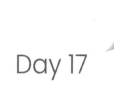

Day 17

BECOMING INTENTIONAL WITH YOUR MIND

READ ROMANS 8

For to set the mind on the flesh is death, but to set the mind on the spirit is life and peace.
—Romans 8:6

It's crazy how specific and direct the Bible really is at times, and yet I often act as if I don't know what to do or how to live out a full, daily Christian life. I think I know better than the Bible and look for wisdom in places it can't be found. Do you? I bet the answer is yes, at least sometimes.

So much of the Christian life is a choice. The work of God through Jesus on the cross is done, and through that death, burial, and resurrection, Jesus has made a way for us, not just for salvation but also to have access to everything we need to do this life in a godly way. (See 2 Peter 1:3.) Romans 8:6 is a wonderful *doing life* principle that can serve us well as we're trying.

Matthew Henry said, "The man is as the mind is." Technically, Romans 8:6 is speaking about the difference between the saved person (spirit) and the unsaved person (flesh), but it isn't a stretch to extend it to what we allow into our minds and how we allow our minds to interpret the world around us. The Bible encourages us, *"Set your minds on things that are above, not on things that are on earth"* (Colossians 3:2).

I'm a reactor. My gut response is to react to the circumstances of life. I can feel it bodily. My heart rate speeds up, my face gets flushed, and I start having *all* the thoughts. All of them—good, bad, and everything in between. In twenty seconds or less, my mind has already contemplated every worst-case scenario and may or may not have tried to convince me they're eminent. Thankfully, I've almost mastered learning not to speak of them aloud until I've had time to process them privately. That's a choice I've realized I need to make that goes against what I'm actually feeling on the inside. It's a choice we all have as the Spirit of God is at work in us.

SOMETHING TO THINK ABOUT

Last summer, my oldest son played baseball against a team he really wanted to beat. He didn't get his wish. More than that, he didn't play very well. Neither did his team. They had the kind of game where everything just seemed to fall apart, and whatever could go wrong...did.

He had a short break in between that game and the next. Our snacks and drinks were out in the car in our cooler, so after the coach finished talking with the team, my son and I walked out of the stadium to the parking lot. I had parked almost at the very back of the parking lot—because doing otherwise at this particular stadium brings the risk of home runs damaging your car—so while we walked the distance, I allowed him to gripe and complain. He talked down about himself, frustrated with his efforts, and bashed himself over his mistakes the entire walk to the car. I didn't say a word. We got our snacks and drinks, and just a few steps away from our car, my son began to complain again.

Clapping my hands loudly, startling my son, I firmly said, "Stop!" I wanted to halt his train of thought abruptly and offer him something different. I said, "Now that we've changed directions, it's time to tell me things you did right or how you will learn from your mistakes in the last game so that you can do something right in the next. I want you to intentionally change your mind, even if you don't feel like it."

He snapped out of the gloom and doom mood he was in and pulled himself together. The entire tone of our conversation changed, and he played better in the next game. If I had allowed him to stay in that depressed, down state, I don't think he would've played any better. Maybe worse.

I know this is a simplified version of a deep biblical truth, but we have a choice about where we allow our minds to take us. If we choose to focus on the things of the flesh—basically anything God calls sinful—we will experience not only possible death as it pertains to our salvation, but death in big and small ways throughout the entire course of our lives. I'm not talking about physical death here, although it could come to that. I'm speaking of a thousand small deaths that result from poor choices to follow what God calls bad instead of intentionally choosing to follow what He calls good—setting our minds on the spirit. A lifetime of moment-by-moment choices for the flesh will result in a path that takes us far from God. On the other hand, a lifetime of intentional, moment-by-moment choices to follow God will lead us right to Him, over and over.

It's not always easy to set our minds on things that bring life, but then nothing we have to intentionally choose for our health and benefit is. The truth is that it's usually easier to set our minds on what leads us from God. In fact, for whatever reason, those thoughts are usually what pop into my head first. But the benefit of learning to set our minds on the spirit leads to life, and that end result far outweighs the cost.

EXTRA VERSES FOR STUDY OR PRAYER

First Corinthians 14:33; Hebrews 13:20

VERSE OF THE DAY

For to set the mind on the flesh is death, but to set the mind on the Spirit is life and peace. —Romans 8:6

PRAYER

Father, it's clear to me from Your Word that I have to intentionally set my mind and thoughts on what You say is true instead of allowing them to be manipulated by what's happening around me. Lord, help me intentionally to do it. In Jesus's name, amen.

THINK

_____

_____

_____

PRAY

_____

_____

PRAISE

_____

_____

_____

TO-DO

_____

_____

_____

PRAYER LIST

_____

_____

_____

QUESTIONS FOR DEEPER REFLECTION

1. What emotions do you experience when your mind is set on things of the world, such as your circumstances, the news, or tragedies?

---

2. How does it feel when you intentionally change directions and force your mind to be set on the things of God, such as His truths, the Bible, and worship?

Day 18

TRAINING FOR PEACE

READ HEBREWS 12

For the moment all discipline seems painful rather
than pleasant, but later it yields the peaceful fruit
of righteousness to those who have been trained by it.
—Hebrews 12:11

Eventually, everyone goes through a life circumstance they'd rather do without. And almost everyone, while in the middle of that circumstance, will ask the question, "Why me?" It's a question I asked almost daily—maybe more than once a day—when my children were very young and hard to handle. It's a question I often asked when my husband couldn't come to church at least twice a month because of shift work. It's a question that rooted itself deeply in my heart for several years as we struggled financially early in our marriage.

I would like to spend our time together today telling you why God chooses to discipline His children, but I can't. I know, on a surface level, that He does it to train us for righteousness or to look more and more like His Son, Jesus. I guess the part I can't really explain is why it has to be this way.

It's a question my oldest son has asked a lot, and the conclusion we come to every time is that sometimes, we just have to make peace with not knowing God's reasons and choosing to trust them anyway. It's not an answer my seventeen-year-old really likes. To be honest, I don't like it either. I wish I could ask God why there isn't another way.

Why, when He *is* the Creator, didn't He design human life so that there was no need for correction, no chance for sin?

Sometimes, we just don't have the answers. That's why it's called faith.

What I do know is that as I look back on the life circumstances that are clearly God's hand of discipline in my life—and even other things that might not have been direct discipline for something I did wrong, but that God used to discipline me nonetheless—I see that I look more like Jesus for them. I'm not saying I enjoyed them. Neither am I saying I'd ask for them again or ask for more in the future. But I've made peace with them because of who they've shaped me to be—a more righteous person who has the peace of being close to Jesus and the firsthand experience of His strong, mighty hands carrying me through them. Now *that* I wouldn't trade.

SOMETHING TO THINK ABOUT

When I find myself asking, "Why me?" I try to do a mental exercise that has helped me have more peace in trying times. I turn the question around and ask, "Why *not* me?" Would I wish my challenges and afflictions on another? Would I rather know Christ *less* and have an easier life?

In Philippians 3, Paul spends a lot of time trying to help us understand just who he was before Christ. I'm not talking about the bad guy called Saul, who killed and persecuted Christians. I'm talking about all of the things he had a right to be proud of, that made him special. Look at this list from verses 4–6:

+ *"Circumcised on the eighth day"* after his birth, which is still important to Jews today

+ *"Of the people of Israel,"* specifically *"the tribe of Benjamin,"* which was known for its courage

+ *"A Hebrew of Hebrews,"* meaning he was purely 100 percent Jewish, and spoke and read Hebrew

+ Zealous

+ A Pharisee

+ Righteous and blameless under the law

And yet, Paul goes on to say:

But whatever gain I had, I counted as loss for the sake of Christ. Indeed, I count everything as loss because of the surpassing worth of knowing Christ Jesus my Lord. For his sake I have suffered the loss of all things and count them as rubbish, in order that I may gain Christ, and be found in him. —Philippians 3:7–9

Wow. Paul suffered much for his unyielding loyalty to Christ, including being stripped of his reputation, physical comfort, relationships, and even basic needs like food and shelter at times. Even if we don't understand why, I pray we'll adopt the same position of the heart and allow God to train us for peace and righteousness.

EXTRA VERSES FOR STUDY OR PRAYER

Psalm 128:6; Colossians 1:20

VERSE OF THE DAY

For the moment all discipline seems painful rather than pleasant, but later it yields the peaceful fruit of righteousness to those who have been trained by it. —Hebrews 12:11

PRAYER

Father, please help me trust You for what's best for me. I confess that I don't always understand, but I do have a desire to place You above all things and know Your worth in my daily life. Help me submit my life and loved ones to Your discipline and to know that You use this discipline to gently make me more like Your Son. In Jesus's name, amen.

THINK

PRAY

PRAISE

TO-DO	PRAYER LIST
_____	_____
_____	_____
_____	_____

QUESTIONS FOR DEEPER REFLECTION

1. Think back to the last time you felt disciplined by the Lord. Was it pleasant? How do you feel about it now?

---

2. How does it make you feel to know that God uses all of your life circumstances to train you and give you the *"peaceful fruit of righteousness"*? How can you apply this to your life?

_____

_____

_____

Day 19

WHY GOD'S PEACE
IS BETTER

READ ROMANS 5

*Therefore, since we have been justified by faith, we have peace
with God through our Lord Jesus Christ.*
—Romans 5:1

It was late at night. I remember that much. Why does the realization of crisis always come late at night? I was lying in bed trying to say my prayers, but instead, I was obsessively running the numbers through my head concerning a big purchase we'd just made. My conclusion wasn't good. In fact, I think I sat up in bed and said to myself, "Why in the world did we do this? This was a bad decision!"

You might wonder why we didn't consider the numbers a bit more before we made our purchase. We had. We'd just forgotten a few things that were right around the corner, like a bump in our car insurance premium because of a new teenage driver (male, which means a *lot* more!), travel baseball dues, and increased costs of living. It was the known unknowns, if you will, that caused a moment of sheer panic, wondering how in the world we were going to make everything work.

Finances are admittedly one of the things that threaten to rob my peace most often in this world. If we have enough money, I feel safe. If we don't, I feel exposed. I still battle living out the truth that God owns it all and will provide for our needs. If I can't see it on paper, it causes me stress, and where stress is, there is no peace.

I tend to want to be able to see peace in real time. This means peace in my finances (enough money), peace in my family (obedient, respectful children), peace in my marriage (a supportive, loving partnership), peace with my friends (agreeable, kind relationships), and peace in my career (a clear vision for the future). Unfortunately, this kind of peace with the *world*, flowing from the outside in, isn't always available. It's what I want, but it isn't always what I get. When I get frustrated, it's because I misunderstand how peace works.

SOMETHING TO THINK ABOUT

Five words in the middle of Romans 5:1 grab my attention: *"We have peace with God."* I won't spend a lot of time on verb tense here because we've already talked about how peace is a fruit of the Spirit, something believers receive along with their decision to follow Christ. Because we have the Holy Spirit living in us, we do have peace. It's just up to us to nurture it on the path toward its growth.

What I want to remind us of with these five words is that peace with God is a peace that comes from within and flows out. It's better than circumstantial peace because our peace with God is the most important kind of peace we can have. Nothing can take it away. Peace with God trumps peace with the world and is a superior perspective from which to look at and understand life.

Unfortunately, most of us spend our lives in pursuit of external peace, believing that it will flow into our hearts and take up residence there. Some of us believe this is the only kind of peace there is or the only kind worth having. But that's a fallacy. Jesus Himself warned us, *"In me you may have peace. In the world you will have tribulation"* (John 16:33).

Christian, the only way we have peace in this troubled, ever-changing world is through our Lord Jesus Christ as we trust in His character, His consistency, and His compassion over what we can see. Sometimes we won't have or be enough. We'll be disrespected, unsupported, undervalued. People will disagree with us and be unkind. More often than not, we'll have just enough vision to put one foot in front of the other on the road to our future, not enough to leap all the way to the top. When the reality that life will be troubled hits, outward peace never makes it to the heart. That's why it's better to focus on the kind of peace that starts in the heart and makes its way out.

EXTRA VERSES FOR STUDY OR PRAYER

Psalm 4:8; Psalm 29:11

VERSE OF THE DAY

Therefore, since we have been justified by faith, we have peace with God through our Lord Jesus Christ. —Romans 5:1

PRAYER

Father, it's only because of You that there's anything good in me. Having peace with You means I can have peace at all times, no matter what the world throws my way. Today, help me remember this truth and thank You for showing me the way to peace. May those I love see it too. In Jesus's name, amen.

THINK

PRAY

PRAISE

_____

_____

_____

TO-DO   PRAYER LIST

_____   _____

_____   _____

_____   _____

QUESTIONS FOR DEEPER REFLECTION

1. How does having peace with God because of Jesus mean you can have peace through anything else?

_____

_____

_____

2. Try to remember a time you were able to have complete peace about something in your world because of the peace you have with God. What was that like? If you've never experienced that kind of peace, what can you do to realize it?

_____

_____

_____

Day 20

WHAT TO DO WHEN YOUR STRENGTH RUNS OUT

READ PSALM 29

May the Lord give strength to his people! May the Lord bless his people with peace!
—Psalm 29:11

When my boys were very little, so young they probably don't remember, I stood with them in front of the ocean and pointed out to the vast, strong, powerful water that filled the horizon to what seemed like its very end. When I had their attention, I said, "See how big and mighty and strong the ocean is? The waves right here on the shore are so strong they knock us over with ease! Can you imagine how much stronger the water is when it gets deeper? The way the water moves, the current, is so strong that I have to come get you when it moves you too far away from me! It's amazing and beautiful and strong and powerful and a little bit scary all at the same time. Do you hear the waves? That sound, and what we know about the ocean, that's what God is like. Psalm 29:3 says, 'The voice of the Lord is over the waters,' and Revelation 1:15 says, 'His voice was like the roar of many waters.' The God we serve—this is who He is. Big, strong, beautiful, and a little overwhelming. But if you listen, you'll hear Him. If you look, you'll see Him. And if you respect Him, He'll be worth it."

Every year, when we go back to the beach, I ask my boys to tell me what God's voice sounds like. If they remember, they'll say, "Like many waters," and I hope it's an association they'll always have. When they look at the water, I hope they feel close to God. I certainly do. I sit in my beach chair under an umbrella and listen to the closest thing to the majesty of the voice of God that I can understand. The idea that His voice is so big and deep and strong fills me with peace that His strength is enough—because mine often, very often, falls short.

I like to be strong. I pride myself on not crying much, and I enjoy feeling like I'm in control. God has gifted each of us with a certain amount of strength. We normally have strength enough to get out of bed and handle what comes our way each day, but despite our very best efforts to do life on our own, there will come a time when our strength runs out. It happened to me when I was twenty-nine. It might happen to you later. But it will happen.

I talk about this in *Unraveled: Hope for the Mom at the End of Her Rope*:

> How many times a day do you catch yourself thinking about what a failure you are, or how your one big mess-up will probably land that little person who watches everything you do straight in the counseling chair a bit later in life? How much of your day do you spend glorifying your weaknesses (dwelling on them, allowing negative internal commentary about them to beat you down) and wondering what will happen if everybody finds out the truth about who you *really* are?[6]

SOMETHING TO THINK ABOUT

I've shared my personal story in other books, so I won't do it again here, but it's important for you to know that motherhood kicked my

---

6. Stacey Thacker and Brooke McGlothlin, *Unraveled: Hope for the Mom at the End of Her Rope* (Eugene, OR: Harvest House Publishers, 2015), 19.

feet right out from under me. Having two boys twenty-three months apart threw me for a major loop, and I spent most of my time in tears, feeling like a complete and utter failure at the one thing I most wanted to get right. I had always been able to work my way into anything I wanted, but not so with motherhood. My strength and personal fortitude served me well until I was about twenty-nine years old.

And then my strength ran out.

It took some wallowing and whining to get there, but eventually, I realized that God's Word says something completely different from what the world tells us about strength. God says our weakness is okay.

In fact, He says it's good. Paul tells us:

> [The Lord] *said to me, "My grace is sufficient for you, for my power is made perfect in weakness." Therefore I will boast all the more gladly of my weaknesses, so that the power of Christ may rest upon me.* —2 Corinthians 12:9–10

In these verses, Paul tells us how to get peace when our strength runs out.

Let it. Let your strength run out. Boast about your weaknesses and then be truly strong. I think God would say something like this to our hearts:

> If you'll let Me, I will make your place of greatest weakness into My place of greatest grace. I'll be the strength you need to keep going, the one who meets you in your mess, the one who leads you to the next right thing and covers your sin. Trust Me. Invite Me in. I have loved you with an everlasting love, and My strength is enough.[7]

EXTRA VERSES FOR STUDY OR PRAYER

Isaiah 41:10; 2 Corinthians 12:1–10

---

7. Ibid., 23.

VERSE OF THE DAY

May the LORD give strength to his people! May the LORD bless his people with peace! —Psalm 29:11

PRAYER

Father, if I rely on my own strength, it will eventually fail. If I try to find my peace outside of You, I will eventually run out. Today and every day, help me remember that my strength is in my relationship with You. You are my true source. In Jesus's name, amen.

THINK

_____
_____
_____

PRAY

_____
_____
_____

PRAISE

_____
_____
_____

TO-DO

_____

_____

_____

PRAYER LIST

_____

_____

_____

QUESTIONS FOR DEEPER REFLECTION

1. Read 2 Corinthians 12:9–10. What does it say about God's strength?

---

2. Have you ever thought about your weaknesses as the perfect opportunity for God to be strong? What does this knowledge do in your heart?

Day 21

PRAYING FOR GOD TO
WORK IN SPITE OF YOU

READ NUMBERS 6:24–26

The Lord bless you and keep you; the Lord make his face to shine upon you and be gracious to you; the Lord lift up his countenance upon you and give you peace.
—Numbers 6:24–26

In our home, Numbers 6:24–26 is known as the *special prayer*. It's been the passage I pray over our children every night before they go to sleep. I started doing it when they were babies, and I've kept doing it almost every night since. When I forget, they ask for it, and my plan is to continue to pray it every day for the rest of *my* life.

I think part of the reason I like to pray this passage so much— and possibly why I choose to pray Scripture most of the time—is because I'm so keenly aware of my lack. I know better than anyone how short I fall as a mom, wife, and child of God. If I made a list of all my weaknesses, I'd never get done, and I'm aware that this lack in me directly affects my children.

In my book *Praying for Boys*,[8] I share the story my dad told me once about a conversation he had with his older brother, my Uncle Bob, at a family picnic. Watching all the cousins talk and hang out,

8. Brooke McGlothlin, *Praying for Boys: Asking God for the Things They Need Most* (Minneapolis, MN: Bethany House Publishers, 2014).

Dad was overcome with emotion. He turned to his brother and asked, "Bob, are they going to turn out okay?" My uncle looked at him and said in reply, "Dave, they're going to turn out okay in spite of us."

I guess that's what I hope I'm praying as I recite our *special prayer*, that God will take our very best, along with everything we didn't get right, and make it into something He can use for His kingdom…in spite of us.

Scripture insists that it's possible. Consider the following biblical characters who came from messed-up backgrounds or experiences and yet were used by God for His purposes:

+ Moses, who killed an Egyptian
+ Rahab, a prostitute
+ Elizabeth, barren until old age
+ Mary, pregnant out of wedlock
+ Peter, publicly denied Christ
+ Paul, a persecutor of Christians

It's clear that *"God chose what is foolish in the world to shame the wise; God chose what is weak in the world to shame the strong"* (1 Corinthians 1:27). These familiar names don't even include the people in my own life whose testimonies have this vibe, my own included. God seems to specialize in making something from nothing, in choosing the foolish to shame the wise or the weak to shame the strong. There can be no doubt that God loves to surprise us, often using people that the rest of the world discounted to accomplish great things.

SOMETHING TO THINK ABOUT

I once shared this quote on Instagram and got a tremendous response: "Be the kind of mom whose kids never know a single day without their mother's prayers." In all seriousness, this one post probably got one of the highest number of likes I've ever gotten. It was inspired by a friend who had posted earlier that day about her son being a senior in high school, and how she and her husband had prayed faithfully for him every day leading up to that time. It really inspired me, and I wanted to share it to inspire others. Mostly it did. However, one mom whose children were already grown and out of the home messaged me privately and said, "I've blown it. It's too late. My children aren't in my home anymore, and I didn't even know about prayer until recently. I feel so defeated."

My heart broke for her, so the next day, I followed up that post with another that said, "It's never too late to become a praying mom." I wanted her and any other mom who felt like she'd missed her chance to know that as long as your kids, or other people you love, are this side of heaven, God can work in their lives through your prayers. God is weaving together the lives and circumstances of all of His children—those who know Him, and those who will know Him one day—to bring about His kingdom plans here on earth. He knows the minute details of each life and exactly what needs to happen in each life to move it toward Him. Our lack may be part of that plan, and we can trust that He'll use it all at just the right time.

EXTRA VERSES FOR STUDY OR PRAYER

First Corinthians 1

VERSE OF THE DAY

The LORD bless you and keep you; the LORD make his face to shine upon you and be gracious to you; the LORD lift up his countenance upon you and give you peace. —Numbers 6:24–26

PRAYER

Father, please bless my loved ones in spite of my lack and the many ways I've failed them and You. I believe You are the Redeemer-God. Redeem anything that's been lost in my life and use it for Your glory. In Jesus's name, amen.

THINK

_____

_____

_____

PRAY

_____

_____

_____

PRAISE

_____

_____

_____

TO-DO   PRAYER LIST

_____   _____

_____   _____

_____   _____

QUESTIONS FOR DEEPER REFLECTION

1. Numbers 6:24–26 is known as the _special prayer_ in my home. Consider making it yours. Pray it now for yourself and your family.

_____

_____

_____

2.   Millions of children around the world do not have the benefit of having a praying mom. Pause for a moment and thank God for the chance you have to be one. If you're not a mom, consider choosing children in need to be your *prayer children* and pray for them on a regular basis.

Day 22

GRACE AND PEACE
TO YOU

READ ROMANS 1:7

To all those in Rome who are loved by God and
called to be saints: Grace to you and peace from God our Father
and the Lord Jesus Christ.
—Romans 1:7

In my last year of school at Virginia Tech, a secular college, I took a New Testament class from a theology professor who I'm not entirely sure was a believer. She never said she was or wasn't. I found that odd at the time because my taking this class coincided with a defining period in my own personal life. It was the first time I'd ever read the entire New Testament from start to finish.

Let's be clear: I did so because I had to—it was a requirement to finish the class—but during that time, the words of the New Testament had also come alive for me in a new way. I had given my heart to Jesus at age nine, but at twenty-one, I began walking with Him closely. This was due, in part, to how God used that class to make His Word real to me like never before. God proved the validity of Hebrews 4:12 as He made the Word *"living and active"* in me. That the professor could have unknowingly been a part of that process, and possibly not even have been changed by it herself, was a mystery to me. I wish I'd told her.

This change in my heart is what I remember most from this class because it changed the course of my entire life. Instead of going on to graduate school in a secular program, I began looking at seminaries and eventually landed on Liberty University's Masters of Professional Counseling program. I wanted to help people, but I wanted to do it with the wisdom of God. It seemed like the perfect fit. That's what made the biggest impression on me from that New Testament class, but the other two memories I have from it were the professor's uncompromising insistence that we spell the names of the books of the New Testament correctly, and what she taught us about Romans 1:7.

According to my best count, seventeen of the twenty-seven New Testament books offer some version of this same salutation from various authors, praying for the recipients to have God's grace and peace. The interesting exception is 2 John 1:3, which says, *"Grace, mercy, and peace will be with us* [not you], *from God the Father and from Jesus Christ the Father's Son."* Even so, the theme of grace and peace is still there.

In today's world, most people barely even say, "Hey!" when sending an email or quick text. Most of the time, we just jump into our short communications without worrying about appropriate social or cultural greetings. Don't even get me started on how my sons intentionally use incorrect grammar and punctuation, choosing not to capitalize letters...ever. It drives me crazy! But in Paul's time, proper greetings were essential, and the most common greeting was simply, "Greetings!" Paul, however, took things a bit further, and in an incredibly significant way, he managed to convey most of the entire Christian theology in a simple opening blessing.

SOMETHING TO THINK ABOUT

This salutation was so important that Paul used it to open every one of his epistles; several other letters that others authored in the New Testament open with it, too. Our Paul shook things up, didn't he? He took a simple, common greeting and turned it into something that would have served as a powerful reminder of just what Jesus did for those he wrote to and who He was to them.

With the word *grace*, Paul said, "Remember that your salvation isn't about you. You didn't earn it. It was given as a gift at great price." (See Ephesians 2:5–8.)

With the word *peace*, Paul said, "Remember that you've been reconciled to God because of Jesus, who paid a great price." (See Ephesians 2:14–17.)

Combined in one greeting, in this specific order, these two words remind the reader that "peace flows *from* grace. We receive well-being and wholeness after having received *grace* from God."[9] In other words, peace comes from the fact that God gave us a gift we didn't deserve. His Son brings our peace.

Grace and peace to you today, friend.

EXTRA VERSES FOR STUDY OR PRAYER

First Corinthians 1:3; 2 Corinthians 1:2; Galatians 1:3; Ephesians 1:2; Philippians 1:2; Colossians 1:2; 1 Thessalonians 1:1; 2 Thessalonians 1:2; 1 Timothy 1:2; 2 Timothy 1:2; Titus 1:4; Philemon 1:3; 1 Peter 1:2; 2 Peter 1:2; 2 John 1:3; Jude 1:2; Revelation 1:4

VERSE OF THE DAY

To all those in Rome who are loved by God and called to be saints: Grace to you and peace from God our Father and the Lord Jesus Christ. —Romans 1:7

PRAYER

Father, thank You for giving me peace through the grace purchased for me at great price through your Son Jesus Christ. Help me to value it appropriately and extend it to others so that they might know You better. In Jesus's name, amen.

9. "Paul's Greeting of 'Grace and Peace,'" *Beyond Today*, September 3, 2019, www.ucg.org/ bible-study-tools/booklets/what-does-the-bible-teach-about-grace/pauls-greeting-of-grace- and-peace.

THINK

_____

_____

_____

PRAY

_____

_____

_____

PRAISE

_____

_____

_____

TO-DO   PRAYER LIST

_____   _____

_____   _____

_____   _____

QUESTIONS FOR DEEPER REFLECTION

1. Have you ever studied the biblical meanings of the words
   grace, *peace*, and *mercy*? If not, take a few minutes to do so.

_____

_____

_____

2. The Bible is fascinating. Learning things like we did today, about how the culture of biblical times affected the way things were written, can help us have a much deeper understanding of what God is trying to communicate to us through the men He used to share His Word. Can you think of other *deeper meanings* like this that God has shown you? If not, start looking for them when you read your Bible.

_____

_____

_____

Day 23

THE PEACE
OF FORGIVENESS

READ COLOSSIANS 3:13

Bearing with one another and, if one has a complaint against another, forgiving each other; as the Lord has forgiven you, so you also must forgive.
—Colossians 3:13

When I was in graduate school, I wrote a research paper on the effects of unforgiveness on people's lives. I wanted to see if a spiritual principle could make its way into our physical and emotional responses. For example, could unforgiveness make us snippy? On edge? Could it damage our relationships with other people? Could it give us headaches? Cause major sickness? Maybe even premature death?

At the Virginia Tech library, I came across the name of a man who has spent much of his career researching forgiveness. Everett Worthington Jr. is a believer and commonwealth professor emeritus at Virginia Commonwealth University. His first book on the topic, *To Forgive Is Human*, had been turned in just before his mother was murdered in 1996. I was amazed at the results of Worthington's research, and he quickly became one of my main sources for my paper.

According to Worthington, unforgiveness is a stress reaction that occurs when there's a perceived wrong or injustice, and it produces many of the same physiological responses as other stressful situations. Sources of stress such as unforgiveness affect our blood pressure, heart rate, breathing, energy levels, sex drive, and even digestion.[10] Over time, Worthington said, unchecked stress can cause issues such as high blood pressure, heart disease, obesity, and diabetes.

Yes, unforgiveness is serious—and not just because of the way it affects us physically. On a spiritual level, it separates us from God. His Word says, *"If you refuse to forgive others, your Father will not forgive your sins"* (Matthew 6:15 NLT). If we don't offer forgiveness to others, we're in danger of having God's forgiveness withheld from us. I'm no theologian, but that doesn't sound good to me.

I'm not saying forgiveness is an easy thing to offer. I personally think Worthington is probably right in distinguishing two types of forgiveness—decisional and emotional. Often, there's a decision to forgive because we know it's the right thing to do or even because we genuinely want to offer it. But in reality, forgiveness often comes in waves. One day, it feels done, and the next day, something painful resurfaces to make it feel like we're starting over from scratch.

I have a friend who experienced sexual abuse as a very young girl at the hands of some teenage boys who thought she was a joke and not worth valuing as a human being. It took years for her to forgive them, and she would tell you that even now, in her early fifties, she still gets triggered by certain events, words, and circumstances. In those times, she chooses to forgive them again, employing decisional forgiveness in hopes that eventually, it will lead to emotional forgiveness.

SOMETHING TO THINK ABOUT

Colossians 3:13 tells us that we should bear with each other and forgive as the Lord forgave us. And while this verse doesn't specifically mention the word *peace*, I can't help but feel that living this way—offering forgiveness on a regular basis, both in small, everyday

10. Everett L. Worthington, Jr. and Michael Scherer, "Forgiveness is an emotion-focused coping strategy that can reduce health risks and promote health resilience: Theory, review, and hypotheses," *Psychology and Health*, June 2004, vol. 19, no. 3, 385–405, greatergood. berkeley.edu/images/uploads/Worthington-ForgivenessCopingStrategy.pdf.

annoyances and in the bigger things that feel like they change our lives—lends itself to a more peaceful existence.

Keeping short accounts, making things right quickly, and even choosing to let small things go can make a huge difference in the peace we feel toward others. *"Love covers a multitude of sins"* (1 Peter 4:8) should be a way of life, not just something we hear of other people doing. Doing the hard work of forgiving in the big things—even if doing so doesn't or can't bring reconciliation—frees up our minds, hearts, and bodies from the physical and emotional stress related to holding onto something that Jesus wants us to release. Forgiveness makes us more and more like Him.

EXTRA VERSES FOR STUDY OR PRAYER

Matthew 6:15; 1 Peter 4:8

VERSE OF THE DAY

Bearing with one another and, if one has a complaint against another, forgiving each other; as the Lord has forgiven you, so you also must forgive. —Colossians 3:13

PRAYER

Father, my human, gut, sinful reaction to injustice against me or someone I love is to bear a grudge and withhold forgiveness, but in reality, it doesn't serve me or Your kingdom to do so. Please give me strength to live at peace with those around me, offering forgiveness in whatever way I can and in Your strength. In Jesus's name, amen.

THINK

PRAY

PRAISE

TO-DO

PRAYER LIST

QUESTIONS FOR DEEPER REFLECTION

1. Have you ever experienced the physical, emotional, and even spiritual ramifications of withholding forgiveness? Have you watched this process happen in someone else? What does it look like?

---

2. Do a heart check. Are you holding onto unforgiveness even now? Go to God and let it go, even if it's hard.

Day 24

PEACE, HOPE, AND LOVE

READ ROMANS 15:13

*May the God of hope fill you with all joy and
peace in believing, so that by the power of the
Holy Spirit you may abound in hope.*
—Romans 15:13

The book of Romans was written by the apostle Paul to bring revival, present true Christian theology and doctrine, and transform lives. Theologians have called it "masterful" and the "chief" of all the epistles. Some have even had the entire book of Romans read to them on a regular basis so they can continue to absorb it and learn from it in old age.

My friend Mary DeMuth, who wrote the foreword for this journal, read the entire book every day for ninety days as she was studying to write about it. That's no small feat. Romans is long, robust, and a bit difficult to follow and understand at times. But it truly is transformative, with many verses making readers come to a full stop. Romans 15:13 is one of those.

I've always found it interesting that Paul chose to use the word *"abound"* in this particular verse. Clearly, he's praying for the people to whom he's writing, which leads me to believe they might not be abounding in hope. I would like to be a person who abounds in hope, but I don't think I am yet, even though I've written two books on the subject. More often, I feel that I have to work at it, fight for it, wait for it, and even pray for God to help me see hope when life's circumstances cloud my view.

Most of the people I've known who seemed to abound in hope were older saints who had lived entire lifetimes with Jesus. One of my favorites was Iris Brammer. She was a fixture in the church I grew up in and ran the public library in our town for so long that it was eventually named after her. By the time I was old enough to be aware of her, she'd been widowed for a long time and was probably in her eighties. She loved children, books, and Jesus…and not in that order. She's the only woman I can remember who was asked to pray publicly during worship service. Her prayers were memorable—long, glowing, passionate responses to the Jesus she loved so much. In fact, as I have matured in my own prayer life, my brother sometimes teases me about being "Mrs. Brammer." I'm honored.

Iris Brammer, as I remember her, brimmed over with hope and the love of Jesus. All of the other people I can think of who have the same demeanor are older, like she was, or found Jesus after going through some major struggles and trials. It makes me think that abounding with hope is something that comes with time and experience, the fruit of a long, deep, and very real walk with the Lord.

SOMETHING TO THINK ABOUT

My friend Stacey Thacker, with whom I wrote those two books on hope, calls hope "the kissing cousin" of joy and peace. It isn't technically one of the fruit of the Spirit listed in Galatians 5:22–23, but it's a fruit of the fruit, if you will. Joy and peace bring hope.

In the Bible, we're told that Jesus is the source of our joy (Habakkuk 3:18), our peace (Ephesians 2:14), and our hope (1 Timothy 1:1). The latter two verses even go as far as to say Jesus *is* our peace and *is* our hope. It's hard to comprehend exactly, but think back to those dreaded word problems from high school. Mathematically, the word *is* means equal to, the exact same thing. This leads me to believe that if Jesus *is* hope and peace, more of Jesus equals more hope, more peace.

In 2012, when Stacey and I first started talking publicly about hope, we had a less-developed understanding of what it looked like and how to get it. We knew it came from Jesus. She would say, "Hope is a person, and His name is Jesus."[11] But now, ten years later, our experiential under-

---

11. Thacker and McGlothlin, *Unraveled*, 47.

standing of hope is so much deeper, richer, and more valuable. Why? Because we've had more of Jesus. We both have experienced major heartaches, struggles, and trials that have proven Jesus to us over and over.

Jesus equals hope. Time and struggle give more Jesus. More Jesus equals abounding hope, joy, and peace.

EXTRA VERSES FOR STUDY OR PRAYER

Habakkuk 3:18; Ephesians 2:14; 1 Timothy 1:1

VERSE OF THE DAY

May the God of hope fill you with all joy and peace in believing, so that by the power of the Holy Spirit you may abound in hope.   —Romans 15:13

PRAYER

Father, the longer I walk with You, the more I believe You are truly my source for hope, peace, and joy. I want to be the kind of person who abounds in hope, but I also know it requires time and trust. Help me to be someone who will work at, fight for, wait for, and pray for more of Your peace, more of You. In Jesus's name, amen.

THINK

_____

_____

_____

PRAY

_____

_____

_____

PRAISE

_____

_____

_____

TO-DO

_____

_____

_____

PRAYER LIST

_____

_____

_____

QUESTIONS FOR DEEPER REFLECTION

1. Do you know someone who abounds in hope? Or joy? Or peace? Think about that person and what you know about their life circumstances. I'm not talking about people who are just naturally positive. I'm talking about people who exude something that is distinctly related to their relationship with Christ. How long have they walked with Jesus? Why does it make a difference?

_____

_____

_____

2. Are you someone who abounds in peace? What do you think it might look like for you to become that person?

_____

_____

_____

Day 25

PEACE IN THE WAITING

READ PSALM 46:10

Be still, and know that I am God. I will be
exalted among the nations, I will be exalted in the earth!
—Psalm 46:10

I once heard it said that there are really no children who don't like to read, only children who are reading the wrong books. I disagree. A lot.

I've been a lifelong reader. In my childhood, my mother made a buffet of classics available to me at all times, as well as some fun books from the early 1990s. (Any other fans of *The Baby-Sitters Club* series out there?) I got books for Christmas, books for my birthday, and books just because. I loved it. To me, getting a new book was an invitation to go live in another world; even though there wasn't anything really wrong with the world I lived in, I loved feeling like a part of something different, even for a little while.

So you can imagine my despair when, despite my very best efforts to do the same thing for my own children, I gave birth to two boys who hate to read. They would have preferred to rip the pages out of books, or use their books as baseball bats, than have to suffer the agony of being still enough to read them. Except at bedtime. They liked to read then, but I'm pretty sure it was only to delay the time when lights went out.

I did everything right. I promise. I created book nooks, bought them beautiful, colorful books, books for boys, books on sports, classics, funny books—you name it, I tried it. I even tried taking them to bookstores to get them excited about books. For me, the simple act of walking into a bookstore produces all kinds of warm, fuzzy feelings. It brings back memories of traveling to the closest bookstore to get the next four or five books in the *Sweet Valley Twins* series when I was twelve. To my sons, however, bookstores were boring.

It took me a while to piece together that when I said it was time to read, my boys heard the words, "It's time to sit still." That, I think, more than anything else, is what they hated. Now that they are teenagers, I have spotted times when they might actually enjoy a book, but they still never read anything other than what their teachers require, and they still hate sitting still.

Metaphorically...spiritually...so do I.

SOMETHING TO THINK ABOUT

In Exodus chapter 14, Moses and the Israelites were fleeing the Egyptian army. Eventually, they found themselves trapped between that army and the Red Sea, and death looked imminent. The Israelites were scared and started to blame Moses for leading them out of their captivity in Egypt to die in the desert. Moses's response is the anthem for anyone in need:

> *Fear not, stand firm, and see the salvation of the* LORD, *which he will work for you today. For the Egyptians whom you see today, you shall never see again. The* LORD *will fight for you, and you have only to be silent.*   —Exodus 14:13–14

Some Bible translations use *"still"* rather than *"silent."*

I think that's the part that bothers me. Not that God will fight for me. Not that He'll provide a way where there doesn't seem to be one. I want that. I'm grateful and humbled by it, especially when I feel hemmed in on every side. It's that I'm supposed to sit still and be quiet while He does it—that's what I don't love. It goes against human nature to be still and let things happen. We want to fix them. It takes commitment and trust to be still in the knowledge that God is God and will take care of our needs. But there's so much more peace available when we do.

EXTRA VERSES FOR STUDY OR PRAYER

Exodus 14

VERSE OF THE DAY

Be still, and know that I am God. I will be exalted among the nations, I will be exalted in the earth! —Psalm 46:10

PRAYER

Father, it's hard for me to wait on You to work, but when I move ahead of You or try to make things happen before the right time—Your time—I make a mess. Help me to not be like the Israelites, fearful and complaining. Instead, help me to wait patiently for You to provide. I believe You always will. In Jesus's name, amen.

THINK

PRAY

PRAISE

_____

_____

_____

TO-DO

_____

_____

_____

PRAYER LIST

_____

_____

_____

QUESTIONS FOR DEEPER REFLECTION

1. Have you ever been in a situation where you were surrounded, so to speak? How did God provide?

_____

_____

2. Do you find it hard to wait and trust God with your circumstances? Where do you think this comes from?

_____

_____

_____

Day 26

PEACE IN KNOWING
WHO GOD IS

READ 2 CORINTHIANS 5:17

*Therefore, if anyone is in Christ, he is a new creation. The old
has passed away; behold, the new has come.*
—2 Corinthians 5:17

Several years ago, I began to remember a sin from my past.
Frequently. It was something God and I had settled a long time ago.
I confessed, meant it, and God gave me freedom from this particular
sin. Not only that, He allowed me a serious victory over it. I've never
felt tempted to sin that way since then, but out of the blue, I found
myself thinking about it almost all the time. When I woke up, it was
the first thing on my mind. At random times throughout the day,
it would pop into my conscious awareness and cause me shame. At
night, when I was trying to pray myself to sleep, it would crowd out
all other thoughts. I couldn't shake it. One night, I felt close to panic
over it and couldn't sleep the whole night.

In the light of day, it was easier to conquer the feelings of guilt
and shame and ask myself why in the world I was struggling so hard
with something so far removed from my current walk with the Lord.
It was done. Under the blood. I was washed clean from this sin.
Forgiven. And yet, here it was. It almost seemed ridiculous to me that
I was even thinking about it again, except for the timing of the attack.

Right before I released my first book, *Praying for Boys*, I began to feel all kinds of pressure, and I had serious doubts about whether any kind of public life—no matter how small it might be—was right for my family. I didn't write *Praying for Boys* from a place of total victory. I wrote it from the perspective of a mom in the trenches who struggled with her boys and had found a *measure* of victory in learning to pray God's Word.

Since then, my measure of victory has increased exponentially, but I still don't write from a position of absolute victory, only as someone who is right there with you in the mess. My boys are the most normal teenagers you'll ever meet. They struggle with the same things almost every other teenage boy struggles with, and they need Jesus just as much as I do.

Right before the book release, I was overwhelmed with the thought that someone who read *Praying for Boys* might expect my boys to be perfect or somehow better, holier, than other boys. Those expectations might hurt them. Was it worth the risk? Should I step back and away from writing books because of the negative impact it could have on my family, on my beloved boys? Those were the questions plaguing me in late 2013.

It was right then, in that crucial moment, that the enemy layered his attack by causing me to remember this sin. I do believe now that it was a strategic attack on me. I don't mean to make myself seem important, but God had given me an important message and a means to share it. Doesn't it make sense that the enemy would want to prevent that? And doesn't it sound just like his tactics to attack me at my weakest points, my children and previous sin?

Believe me, the enemy will attack you no matter who you are, even if you're not in full-time ministry. You just need to be following God's will, working for His kingdom, or praying for others on the front lines. That is fulfilling the Great Commission of Matthew 28:19–20.

SOMETHING TO THINK ABOUT

I've learned that when the enemy reminds me of who I *was*, I remind him of *who God is*. That reminds him of *who I am now*.

I believe the enemy was trying to keep me from following what I know God had called me to do in that season. He tried to make me feel like it would endanger my family and tried to make me question whether I was qualified because of previous sin. The truth is that radically following Jesus can be dangerous. Truth be told, I'm probably the least qualified person I know to do anything for God at all. But I think that's what might actually qualify me. And you.

When the enemy wants to throw what happened before you knew Jesus in your face, remind him of Who you belong to now. The only thing we *must* have to qualify for the right to work in His kingdom is His forgiveness. And we have that.

EXTRA VERSES FOR STUDY OR PRAYER

First Corinthians 1:27

VERSE OF THE DAY

Therefore, if anyone is in Christ, he is a new creation. The old has passed away; behold, the new has come.

—2 Corinthians 5:17

PRAYER

Father, thank You *so* much for making me new. All of my sin—past, present, and future—is covered by the sacrifice of Your Son. *I am covered.* When the enemy tries to remind me of who I used to be, help me remember to tell him who *You are.* In Jesus's name, amen.

THINK

PRAY

PRAISE

TO-DO

PRAYER LIST

QUESTIONS FOR DEEPER REFLECTION

1. Do you think of yourself as a new creation? What does it mean to you to know that the old has passed away?

2. Does the enemy attack you with what once was? Remind him of what is.

Day 27

PEACE IN ABIDING

READ 1 JOHN 2:24

Let what you heard from the beginning abide in you.
If what you heard from the beginning abides in you, then you
too will abide in the Son and in the Father.
—1 John 2:24

The past few weeks at the McGlothlin Home for Boys—as I've affectionately called our home for the last fifteen years—have reminded me that I'm raising two normal, challenging, beautiful boys. At almost fifteen and seventeen, one with a new driver's license, they are spending more and more time away from our home. Sports, time with friends, girlfriends (gasp!), church activities, and more threaten our time with them on a regular basis. And I'm not complaining. They are getting ready to be men. My oldest is a senior this year, and we're talking to friends and family who work in the profession he's interested in to figure out next steps.

Next. Steps.

How did we get here? When I wrote *Praying for Boys*, they were five and seven years old, and I wasn't sure I would survive them! In fact, I had realized I wouldn't without God's help, which is why I wrote the book. I look back now at all the times my husband and I have poured into them, prayed over them, taught them the Scriptures, and taken them to church, and I can see how quickly it all goes by.

And I'm left with this one prayer: "Lord, let it stick."

While I was working concessions at a basketball game recently, a teacher at my sons' school approached me to tell me that my oldest is a good boy. Her son had attended a Fellowship of Christian Athletes meeting after lunch the week before, and my son was the speaker. Just for a few minutes. Probably less than five. But whatever he'd shared stuck with her son enough that he shared it with his mom. And she felt compelled to speak to me.

SOMETHING TO THINK ABOUT

My son *is* a good boy. But he can also be silly and a little bit of a class clown. Really, he's a completely normal teenager with doubts, fears, and questions about life and faith. It's important to me that you know that. My boys are normal, and the fears I face as a mom are most likely the same as yours. Many, *many* mornings, I've watched him ride down our driveway with his brother and prayed, "Lord, let it stick." What I mean by that is, "Lord, please take everything we've done and said and let the truth of it all be what whispers in their ears when they're away from us. Let what they've heard from the beginning abide in them."

My prayer is that the truth of God's Word that we've tried to hide in their hearts over the course of their lives has rooted itself so deeply that it comes out when they least expect it—to guide them, control them, inspire them, and lead them. As a mom, I can spend all my time worrying about the challenges they'll face and the temptations they'll have to overcome, or I can trust that God's Word won't return void in their lives. (See Isaiah 55:11.) We've been faithful to share it with them and to help them understand it, and we have fervently prayed it over their lives almost since birth. God will keep those seeds of faith safe and help them grow in just the right time. I believe it, and this brings me peace.

EXTRA VERSES FOR STUDY OR PRAYER

Isaiah 55:11–13; Hebrews 4:12

VERSE OF THE DAY

Let what you heard from the beginning abide in you. If what you heard from the beginning abides in you, then you too will abide in the Son and in the Father. —1 John 2:24

PRAYER

Father, my children, my loved ones...they belong to You. Help me to be a faithful witness in their lives and let what I've planted in their hearts from the beginning abide in them, growing deep and fruitful roots. In Jesus's name, amen.

THINK

_____

_____

_____

PRAY

_____

_____

_____

PRAISE

_____

_____

_____

TO-DO

_____

_____

_____

PRAYER LIST

_____

_____

_____

QUESTIONS FOR DEEPER REFLECTION

1. Have you faithfully shared your faith with your kids? If not, start today. It might feel weird to everyone for a while, but kids are more resilient and forgiving than you might think. Take a step of faith and share Jesus with them today!

------

2. When things go wrong with our kids, we can feel tempted to be overwhelmed and feel like failures in everything. Take a moment to make a list of the things you've done *right* with your kids and then thank God for it, asking Him to take the seeds of faith and grow them in your children's hearts.

Day 28

PEACE IN COMMUNITY

READ 1 CORINTHIANS 10:13

*No temptation has overtaken you that is not common to man.
God is faithful, and he will not let you be tempted beyond your
ability, but with the temptation he will also provide the way of
escape, that you may be able to endure it.*
—1 Corinthians 10:13

It always helps me to know I'm not alone.

When my boys were really little, I felt extremely isolated. Not because I didn't have friends, or a church family, or even my own family to turn to. Mainly, I felt isolated because I was afraid to let people see how much I was struggling as a mom. I didn't feel like I was doing a good job, and my goal-oriented, perfectionistic self thought I had to hide it.

To be honest, it wasn't all about trying to hide. Sometimes I really felt like people didn't understand my children—two hard-to-handle, loud, aggressive boys—and I wanted to take the time we had at home to work and grow in hopes that it would spill over into our public life. But it still kept me away from others, alone with my thoughts.

Regardless of the reasons, the result was that I felt isolated. Because of that, I also felt like I was the only mom who struggled with her kids. Reread what I just said. Because of my difficulties, I felt like I was the only mom who struggled with her kids.

I know now that this was a lie, but back then, that lie felt like the truest of truths, and I struggled to get out from under it. As a result, my weaknesses began to be all I could see. They got so big that I felt like a miserable failure. That way of thinking—that things were never going to be right, and I didn't have what it took—began to permeate my heart and soul. Thinking this way caused me to see all the bad in my life very easily, but made it much more difficult to see the good. It's a pessimistic way of life and not very fun. I found my sons' early childhood years to be very stressful and lacking in peace.

If you'd asked me back then to make a list of my weaknesses, I could've taken up two pages in two minutes flat. I knew where I lacked, but I wasn't sure what to do about it. On the other hand, had you asked me to make a list of my strengths, I might've struggled. Motherhood caused me to question myself a lot. It shook me up and kicked my feet out from under me in all the right ways. I look back now and I know…

I needed to be shaken.

SOMETHING TO THINK ABOUT

God used motherhood to totally reorient my thinking. I find that He does that for most of us, whether we're moms or not. Because He loves us so much, He's unwilling for us to remain the way we are, or to think about life with a perspective that is any less His. Doing so ruins us. It's truly a big deal to look at life through the lens of anything other than God's Word. Because He was so kind to me, He shook me loose and caused me to let go of ways of thinking about myself and others that weren't doing me any good, including the lie that I was the only mom who struggled.

Part of the answer to this, for me, was to step out into the sunshine. Into community. I started intentionally surrounding myself with women who were further along in their motherhood and life journey, and I watched them live. I observed their choices, got into Scripture with them at women's Bible studies, and even led a few

Bible studies myself. It isn't an understatement to say that it changed my life to see that other women struggled. In *Unraveled*, I wrote:

> I chose to fill the empty spaces of a weary mom's life with truth instead of complaining, faith instead of fretting, grace instead of comparison. I stopped listening to the voices that pointed out my shame and beat me down and started filling my heart with the voices of truth.[12]

The other part was learning to recognize that I actually don't have what it takes. I'm not enough. I won't ever be enough, and I can stop trying to be enough. I began to be okay with not having all the answers and going to the One who does. I realized:

> Whatever strengths and weaknesses we possess are all a part of God's plan for our beautiful, messy lives. He uses every detail of our mess for His greater glory and can redeem even our deepest, darkest, most daring mistakes until they're more beautiful than we could've ever imagined.[13]

EXTRA VERSES FOR STUDY OR PRAYER

First Corinthians 12:14–18; 2 Corinthians 12:9–10

VERSE OF THE DAY

No temptation has overtaken you that is not common to man. God is faithful, and he will not let you be tempted beyond your ability, but with the temptation he will also provide the way of escape, that you may be able to endure it. —1 Corinthians 10:13

PRAYER

Father, help me to remember that I'm not alone. Even when I struggle in life, even if I can't find a mentor, and even if

---

12. Thacker and McGlothlin, *Unraveled*, 22.
13. Ibid., 23.

community is scarce, I still have You. Help me to not hide from You and to be okay with not having all the answers because *You* have them. In Jesus's name, amen.

THINK

_____
_____
_____

PRAY

_____
_____
_____

PRAISE

_____
_____
_____

TO-DO   PRAYER LIST

_____   _____
_____   _____
_____   _____

QUESTIONS FOR DEEPER REFLECTION

1. It is not an easy thing to pull the curtains back on all that isn't right about our lives. Believe me, I know! But it does bring relief to find that we're not alone, and that other people struggle in the same ways we do. Do you need to pull the curtain back on something today?

_____

_____

_____

2. How can you join a community of like-minded women? If you can't find one, could you start one?

_____

_____

_____

Day 29

PEACE FOUND IN THE TRUTH

READ JOB 9:4-6

For God is so wise and so mighty. Who has ever challenged him successfully? Without warning, he moves the mountains, overturning them in his anger. He shakes the earth from its place, and its foundations tremble.
—Job 9:4–6 (NLT)

Sometimes, God doesn't move the mountain.

I know, I know. I love the song "Mighty to Save,"[14] too, and it just wouldn't have the same ring if they sang, "Savior, He can move the mountains, but sometimes He chooses not to." However, it's the truth. God can absolutely move any mountain in our lives...but sometimes, He chooses something different.

Recently, my two teenagers and I sat around the table and discussed what it really means to fall away from God. We talked about how everyone, at times, gets mad at God, questions Him, and maybe even stops talking to Him for a while. Some will choose to never return to God, but I believe those people may not have truly known the Lord to begin with. Others, like Peter, will say:

---

14. Hillsong Worship, "Mighty to Save," on *Mighty to Save* (Hillsong Music, 2006).

Lord, to whom shall we go? You have the words of eternal life, and we have believed, and have come to know, that you are the Holy One of God.   —John 6:68–69

For a brief time in my thirties, I stopped believing God wanted to be good to me. We'd endured a series of heartbreaks as a family, culminating with an early miscarriage of our third child. I was left stunned and, truthfully, a little bit frustrated that God had not moved any of the mountains that presented themselves in our lives over the past several years. I spent a few months not praying, not really reading my Bible, and not talking to anyone about how I was feeling. But in the end, I found my way back, in part because of what Peter said.

I became a Christian when I was nine years old and began walking closely with the Lord days before my twenty-first birthday. I had a genuine relationship with Jesus. I *knew* the truth. I knew that Jesus had the words of eternal life, and I had believed, sincerely, that He was the Holy One of God. Once you *know* that, deep down in your heart, it's my belief that you can't unknow it, even if God doesn't move your mountains.

SOMETHING TO THINK ABOUT

Having faith in what God can do is good. Belief is good. Praying for God to remove obstacles in our lives isn't bad. But our faith, our belief, and our prayers aren't what move mountains. They aren't magical, and we don't get to choose the mountains that get moved. Our faith, our belief, and our prayers partner with God, who made the mountain and can make it move if He so chooses. And sometimes He doesn't. Sometimes He asks us to walk around it. Sometimes He asks us to hike over it. Sometimes He asks us to tunnel through it. Sometimes He asks us to just sit with it for a while so we can learn to comfort those dealing with the same mountain. (See 2 Corinthians 1:4.) Sometimes we never get rid of it because God is using it to keep us desperate for Him. (See 2 Corinthians 12:9.)

I don't always understand that. I don't know why different people get different paths—over, around, or through their mountain—and I wish I could figure out a rhythm or pattern to make it all fit. If there is one, it belongs to God, and He alone decides what to do with my mountains and yours.

This isn't necessarily the message we want to hear, but it's a true one. And knowing the truth changes our experience of the love and goodness of God. This means everything. So keep asking God to move the mountain, whatever it is. I plan to. But know that if He doesn't move it for you, it just means your mountain is right where He wants it to be for now—and so are you.

EXTRA VERSES FOR STUDY OR PRAYER

First Corinthians 1; 2 Corinthians 12

VERSE OF THE DAY

For God is so wise and so mighty. Who has ever challenged him successfully? Without warning, he moves the mountains, overturning them in his anger. He shakes the earth from its place, and its foundations tremble. —Job 9:4–6 (NLT)

PRAYER

Father, You are good. No matter what happens in my life, whether You move my mountains or leave them there for Your glory, You're good. Help me to trust You even in this. In Jesus's name, amen.

THINK

PRAY

_____

_____

_____

PRAISE

_____

_____

_____

TO-DO

_____

_____

_____

PRAYER LIST

_____

_____

_____

QUESTIONS FOR DEEPER REFLECTION

1. Has God ever not moved a mountain for you? What did that feel like?

_____

_____

_____

2. Have you ever considered that God's decision to leave your mountain might've been what was best for you or for someone else in your life?

_____

_____

_____

Day 30

PEACE IN BEING ABLE TO PRAY

READ PSALM 23

Yea, though I walk through the valley of the shadow of death,
I will fear no evil: for thou art with me;
thy rod and thy staff they comfort me.
—Psalm 23:4 (KJV)

One of the most annoying prayer clichés to me is, "Well, all we can do is pray." For years, I've believed that most Christians get this backwards. Prayer is not a last resort. It's the first and best response we have to the challenges of life. I believe with all my heart that God designed prayer as our way of partnering with Him, having a relationship with Him, and working with Him to accomplish His kingdom purposes here on earth. There are a lot of things about prayer I don't understand, but this I do believe: prayer is not a cop-out. It's not passive. And it's not a last resort. Prayer is action, and it's what we should turn to first.

That said, there are times when all we can do is pray. However, that knowledge should fill us with peace, hope, and renewed strength, not depression or desperation.

Let's change the way we think about prayer. We have access to the *God who can!* Prayer is something we *get* to do! It's the privilege and right of believers to ask God to act when others must rely only on their own strength. When we truly have faith in the God who can, there's no need to let the fact that we often *can't* steal our peace.

Maybe you've experienced a heartbreak, challenge, or diagnosis that you literally have no power to change. Maybe there's a relationship you can't fix, and this knowledge makes you feel sad and powerless.

Lift up your head.

Maybe your life doesn't look like you dreamed it would, or God hasn't answered a prayer the way you expected. Maybe He has felt silent on a subject of the utmost importance to you and simply hasn't yet made a way for what you need.

Lift up your head.

Maybe when you look closely at the story of your life, it seems impossible that you've lived through the difficulties and trials, and you wonder how the woman looking back at you changed so much from the girl you used to be.

Lift up your head.

As a believer, a child of God, prayer may actually be the only thing we can do in certain situations, but we have a hope unbelievers do not. Even when you feel like there's nothing more to be done, nothing more you can do to fix the hurts in your life, or change the way things turned out, you are not without strategy. God has given you access to Himself. And while He might not choose to fix it immediately, or in the way you desire, there is always hope when you partner with Him.

Lift up your head!

SOMETHING TO THINK ABOUT

The mystery of prayer, my dear friend, is that it's so much more than just a simple yes, no, or wait. It *is* these things. God *does* answer us when we cry out to Him. But prayer is the way we talk to the God who created us, loves us, sent His Son to die for us, and desires a personal, intimate relationship with us. Prayer is what makes the believer different from any other person of any other faith. Prayer may not be unique to the Christian faith, but as Christians, we have the distinction of praying to the *only* God who conquered death, who is still alive and actively guiding and loving His disciples from a position of power and glory in heaven.

Prayer is active faith in the God who gives us everything we need, for every situation we encounter. Prayer is getting more of God Himself. Not always the answer we hoped for, but always more of God.

That's what you have. Not desperation. Not hopelessness. Not a last resort. But the ability to confidently move forward in peace, knowing you're not alone. *You are never alone.*

SOMETHING TO PRAY

The Lord is my shepherd; I shall not want. He maketh me to lie down in green pastures: he leadeth me beside the still waters. He restoreth my soul: he leadeth me in the paths of righteousness for his name's sake. Yea, though I walk through the valley of the shadow of death, I will fear no evil: for thou art with me; thy rod and thy staff they comfort me. Thou preparest a table before me in the presence of mine enemies: thou anointest my head with oil; my cup runneth over. Surely goodness and mercy shall follow me all the days of my life: and I will dwell in the house of the Lord forever.   —Psalm 23:1–6 KJV

EXTRA VERSES FOR STUDY OR PRAYER

Second Peter 1:3

VERSE OF THE DAY

Yea, though I walk through the valley of the shadow of death, I will fear no evil: for thou art with me; thy rod and thy staff they comfort me.   —Psalm 23:4 (KJV)

PRAYER

Father, thank You for wanting to give me more of Yourself. In the times when I'm tempted to despair and even in the times when all is going well, help me to remember that I'm never alone, never without hope, and never without wisdom, if I'll simply cry out to You in prayer. In Jesus's name, amen.

THINK

_____

_____

_____

PRAY

_____

_____

_____

PRAISE

_____

_____

_____

TO-DO   ## PRAYER LIST

_____   _____

_____   _____

_____   _____

QUESTIONS FOR DEEPER REFLECTION

1. What's your prayer life like? Do you pray often, or treat it like it's a last resort?

   _____

   _____

   _____

2. All of us can improve our prayer life. If yours isn't what you want it to be, choose one thing you can do to invite God into the moments of your day. Consider setting your alarm for a certain time and pausing for a few minutes to pray.

   _____

   _____

   _____

ABOUT THE AUTHOR

Brooke McGlothlin received her B.S. in psychology from Virginia Tech and her master's degree in counseling from Liberty University. For over ten years, she served as director of clinical services in a local pregnancy care ministry before making the best choice of her life—to stay home with her boys. Brooke uses her ministry experience to reach women, writing to bring hope to the messes of life in the midst of her own messy life.

In 2010, Brooke cofounded Raising Boys Ministries with Erin Mohring and equipped parents of boys to raise godly men for over nine years. In 2019, they launched a new ministry, Million Praying Moms, which exists to help moms make prayer their first and best response to the challenges of parenting.

Brooke now leads Million Praying Moms solo and hosts the Million Praying Moms podcast. You can find her writing and creating prayer resources for today's Christian moms at the Million Praying Moms blog. Her books include *Praying for Boys: Asking God for the Things They Need Most*; *Unraveled: Hope for the Mom at the End of Her Rope*; *How to Control Your Emotions, So They Don't Control You: A Mom's Guide to Overcoming*; *Gospel Centered Mom: The Freeing Truth About What Your Kids Really Need*; and *Praying Mom: Making Prayer the First and Best Response to Motherhood*.

Brooke, her husband, and their two sons make their home in the mountains of Appalachia, calling southwestern Virginia home.

To connect with Brooke, visit:

www.millionprayingmoms.com

www.brookemcglothlin.net